JIM HANCOCK & KARA POWELL

GOOD SEX

LEADER'S GUIDE
A WHOLE-PERSON APPROACH TO TEENAGE SEXUALITY AND GOD

2.0

ZONDERVAN®

ZONDERVAN.com/
AUTHORTRACKER
follow your favorite authors

youth
specialties

ZONDERVAN

Good Sex 2.0: A Whole-Person Approach to Teenage Sexuality and God
Copyright 2009 by Jim Hancock and Kara Powell

Youth Specialties resources, 300 S. Pierce St., El Cajon, CA 92020 are published by Zondervan, 5300 Patterson Ave. SE, Grand Rapids, MI 49530.

ISBN 978-0-310-28271-6

Cover and interior design by SharpSeven Design

Printed in the United States of America

CONTENTS

INTRODUCTION | README

It doesn't take a genius to see we're raising kids who feel upside down about sex. And it's no secret that the Church has lost her voice, partly from confusion and fear, and partly from screaming herself hoarse. Those of us who aren't scared silent suffer a sort of cultural laryngitis: people see our lips moving but can't always make out what we're saying.

Wouldn't it be nice to have a reasonable, direct, honest, genuine, hopeful conversation about sex? Wouldn't it be good for our kids to hear us speak of God's good gifts in glowing, optimistic terms? Wouldn't it be wonderful to talk about sex without fear or anger or pretense?

We can, if we really want to. *Good Sex* is presented with that hope.

Here are some big ideas behind *Good Sex*:
- We're created in God's image, male and female.
- Sexuality is a wonderful, complex gift that takes a lifetime to explore.
- Sex touches every part of us—our bodies, sure, but also our minds, emotions, spirits, and every relationship, from our families to the God who makes us sexual (and everyone in between).
- Sex is affected by our brokenness and wrongdoing, just like everything else about us.
- Sex can be rescued and renewed by the grace of Christ, just like everything else about us.

Good Sex helps kids look at sex in the broad context of their whole lives. More precisely, *Good Sex* helps *youth workers*—pros, semi-pros, and volunteers—help students understand sex in the context of their whole lives.

Good Sex is organized into seven sessions:

- **Sex Messaging**: helping kids respond to the cultural messages they're wading through (or maybe more accurately, swimming in)
- **Sexual Identity**: helping kids think about the forces that shape their sexuality
- **Intimacy**: helping kids think about dating and nonsexual closeness
- **Desire**: helping kids understand their appetites and needs
- **Boundaries**: helping kids decide what to do with their sexuality
- **Responsibility**: helping kids take sexual responsibility
- **Do-Overs**: helping kids experience mercy, repentance, forgiveness, and restoration

Each session includes a "Suggested Session Outline" that you can complete from beginning to end. It follows three steps:[1]

NOW | What is really happening with your students' sexuality right now?

NEW | What new perspective can we glean from Scripture?

HOW | How do we want to live differently?

We've tried to make this organization clear enough that you can hand it to a volunteer who has about 20 minutes to prepare. Then she can use it in a small group while you're off at a health spa (praying for her, of course). At the same time, we've tried to make it flexible enough that you or another leader can prayerfully and intentionally customize it to your own setting.

The "Suggested Session Outline" is followed by a collection of "Other Resources for Teaching" on that topic. Think of the "Suggested Session Outline" as our daily special—a tasty, balanced meal served up with all the trimmings. And think of the "Other Resources for Teaching" as ordering off the menu. More on this in a moment.

---

1. These steps are adapted from the Deep Design presented in *Deep Ministry in a Shallow World* and *Deep Justice in a Broken World* by Chap Clark, Kara E. Powell, and the Center for Youth and Family Ministry.

There's a logic to the order of the seven lessons, but the table of contents does *not* reflect a hard-and-fast conviction about the order in which the material should be covered.

Sex Messaging is a relatively low-risk place to start compared with, say, **Desire** or **Do-Overs**. It's located at the beginning to give you a chance to assess what your group knows and thinks and how ready they are for some of the more challenging material.

Do-Overs is somewhat more challenging because it deals with sexual brokenness. So we put it at the end. But don't withhold the good news about God's restoration if you sense it ought to be included in lesson one (or three times in session four!). "If we confess our sins," John says, God is "faithful and just and will forgive us our sins and purify us from all unrighteousness" (1 John 1:9). Rely on it.

Now, back to the program elements called "Other Resources for Teaching on (Whatever)." You may be wondering, *Why create a bunch of extra resources that aren't part of a lesson plan? Why complicate things?* We're glad you asked...

The simple answer is that we know youth groups, but we don't know *your* youth group. We don't know your theology, your history, your gifts, your skills, your community; and we don't know your boss. There's a lot we don't know. What we *do* know is, the more experienced you are, the more likely it is you'll take whatever we do and rearrange it to fit your situation. You have to. We know that because that's what we've done with youth ministry resources for years. These "Other Resources" aren't leftovers. They're as good as—and for your purposes, maybe even better than—what we've included in the "Suggested Session Outline." If you see something in the lesson plan that doesn't bowl you over, replace it with something that does (as if you needed our permission to do that...).

Here's the more complicated answer:

In the real world, kids encounter sexual information and experiences in a process that stretches over decades. Most of that information and quite a bit of the experience is indirect. They read, listen, watch television and movies, and hang out with friends and acquaintances. They watch their parents and other adults. They watch their siblings and other peers. They experience sexual arousal (and it takes them by surprise).

From all these impressions, they construct a picture of what sex is—or appears to be. And out of that picture come their sexual attitudes, opinions, and actions. The picture is updated as they encounter new information and experiences and, even in adulthood, the picture is never complete as long as they're learning.

Contrast that with most teaching (as distinct from *learning*) about sex. Most of what kids get directly from adults is much less a *process* and much more a *confrontation*: "Here are the facts, remember them. These are the boundaries, don't cross them. This is the truth, believe it."

If we agree that experience is the best teacher (not the preferred teacher, perhaps, but the most effective), then which of these seems likely to be more influential: *process* or *confrontation*? We believe *Good Sex* should be more a process than a confrontation because we believe that's how people really learn.

"Well, we can't always talk about love, sex, and dating," you say.

Why not? Once they reach puberty, kids are always talking about relationships with the other gender. They're exposed to films, books, magazines, games, Web sites, music, and television shows that constantly talk about sexuality. They live in a human context that's always, on one level or another, about sex. It's all part of the process. Except at church (and a few other adult-sensitive settings), where grown-ups typically *confront* instead of *process*. Come to think of it, the confrontation teenagers usually get from adults becomes *part* of the larger process, whether or not it's a conscious choice. That's one reason kids don't believe it's safe to talk about sex when adults are in the room.

An ancient Hebrew liturgy celebrates this *process* of leading kids into loving obedience to their invisible Creator. This liturgy, called *Shema* (shay-máh), says, in part:

> Hear, O Israel: The Lord our God, the Lord is one. Love the Lord your God with all your heart and with all your soul and with all your strength. These commandments that I give you today are to be on your hearts. Impress them on your children. Talk about them when you sit at home and when you walk along the road, when you lie down and when you get up. Tie them as symbols on your hands and bind them on your foreheads. Write them on the doorframes of your houses and on your gates. (Deuteronomy 6:4-9)

That's process. The same sort of process the other guys—the ones whose values we don't share—employ, whether they mean to or not. If you want to impress the next generation with biblical values around sex, then it's the way we're recommending you do it, too.

We don't believe an annual sex talk or even the old six-week series with a concluding abstinence pledge goes far enough to help kids wrestle with (and finally get pinned by) what the Bible says about sexuality. We believe sex demands to be included in youth ministry as a subtext throughout the year—it's certainly a subtext in kids' lives, and they face new questions all the time.

Allow us to make a few suggestions on how *Good Sex* can help you do that.

First, on the accompanying DVD, you'll find all the reproducible handouts referenced in each of the sessions—they'll help students personalize what they're learning in various elements throughout the session. You can print them out, make copies, and use them to enhance large group discussion, or as more intimate small group conversation starters (or finishers), or as a tool for students' individual personal reflection. You can tell which elements come with handouts by reading the "You'll need—" box at the start of each element.

This probably goes without saying, but the degree to which you integrate the handouts, as well as the way you use them, will affect how much time each element takes (not to mention your teaching style and the way students respond to the discussion). So although we've offered time estimates for each element, please note that they may not apply in your setting.

Second, on the accompanying DVD, you'll find all the transcripts of the DVD video segments in case you want to follow along with them in writing or have students act out the clips instead of watching them.

Third, we recommend spreading out the program elements from "Other Resources for Teaching" across your year: 10 minutes here, an evening there, wherever it fits the larger process of youth ministry to the whole person. Once you start thinking about it, you'll probably see a host of topics that relate to sexuality: family relationships, emotions, school, temptation, peer pressure, the media—the list goes on and on.

Fourth, we created a book for kids called *What (almost) Nobody Will Tell You About Sex*. It's a process-centered resource that invites kids to consider, understand, and surrender their sexuality to the God who loves them and made them sexual.

Fifth, draw from the sidebars sprinkled throughout the book as liberally or conservatively as you'd like. Some of these tidbits reflect the most recent research findings related to adolescent sexuality; others help you (and maybe your students) dive deeper into the Scriptures; still others are quotations that we just liked.

Sixth, be a participant as much as you can. If you're not processing your own sexual experiences, it's tough to help kids go all the way (forgive the pun) in processing theirs. That's why we've included a process called "For Your Own Preparation" at the beginning of each chapter. It's the stuff we hope you'll be thinking about as you lead students in understanding their sexuality.

Seventh, pull from **The Stuff at the Back of the Book** as needed, including "Plumbing + Wiring FAQs," "Back-to-Basics Biology," "All the Sex in the Bible," and especially "How to Help Victims of Sexual Abuse and Other Tough Stuff."

We're awfully glad you're where you are—serving God and serving kids. We believe the opportunity and obligation to speak into the lives of adolescents as they understand and offer their sexuality to the God who made them is a sacred trust. *Good Sex* is our humble contribution to that conversation. We pray it will help you help kids grow into whole and healthy people who love God with everything in them and love their neighbors as they love themselves.

90-MINUTE PARENT MEETING:
TALKING TO YOUR KIDS ABOUT SEX

In the midst of planning to teach about *Good Sex*, please don't make the all-too-common mistake of forgetting about—or hiding from—your students' parents. When it comes to teenagers' sexual choices, their parents are far more influential than even the most dedicated youth worker. Because youth workers tend to avoid meeting with parents—and because when youth workers *do* sit down with parents, they usually wing it—we've given you this plan for a 90-Minute Parent Meeting. Use it as a springboard to create the type of discussion you'd like to have with parents.

NOW (20 minutes)

Welcome parents and ask them to introduce themselves to the group and share the names and ages of their children.

Explain: **Your coming here tonight shows me that you hope to avoid one of the major mistakes some parents make when it comes to their kids' sexuality: failing to talk with them about it. Many times we're afraid that our kids won't talk to us at all. Other times we're equally afraid that they *will* talk to us and we won't like what we hear.**

> You'll need—
> • A copy of the movie *What Women Want* (Paramount, 2000), cued to 1:18:18
> • A television or video projection unit
> • A DVD player
> • A whiteboard or poster paper
> • Pens

At this point set up the *What Women Want* clip by explaining that Nick Marshall (played by Mel Gibson) is sitting in a restaurant with his teenage daughter (played by Ashley Johnson), trying to talk to her about sex. Nick is divorced and doesn't live with his daughter, which adds to the awkwardness. Also explain that, following an accident, Nick now has the uncanny ability to hear women's thoughts, including his own daughter's.

Play the clip and stop the DVD at 1:20:25 when Nick rests his head in his hands and says, "Please."

Q: How do you think Nick is feeling as he talks with his daughter about sex? What do you think is motivating him to bring up the subject?

Q: If you could read your teenagers' thoughts when you've tried to talk with them about sex (for those of you who have), what would they be thinking?

(For the next two questions, write the parents' answers on a whiteboard or poster paper.)

Q: What obstacles prevent Nick and his daughter from having a good talk about sex?

Q: What other obstacles keep us from having productive, authentic conversations about sex with our kids?

NEW (40 minutes)

Explain: **The obstacles that keep parents from having good conversations with their kids about sex tend to come from both sides of the relationship (meaning from both parents and kids). Today we're going to discuss how to overcome both types of obstacles so we can start having more healthy and authentic conversations with our kids.**

Overcome Your Own Obstacles as Parents by Realizing...

1. YOU'RE MORE INFLUENTIAL THAN YOU THINK. Explain: **Given the media's messages about the influence of friends on our kids' sexual choices, we often forget the importance of our own words, actions, and attitudes as parents. A 2004 National Campaign to Prevent Teen Pregnancy study asked parents who they thought had the most influence on their teens' sexual choices. Close to half of the parents thought their teens' *friends* had the most influence. Here's the good news: in reality, 45 percent of teenagers ages 12 to 14 said *parents* were the most influential, with friends coming in a distant second at 31 percent.[2]**

Similarly, a national survey of almost 15,000 seventh through twelfth graders found that kids who perceived that their parents disapproved of teenage sexual activity were less likely to become sexually active.[3] One study of more than 1,000 12-to-16-year-olds found that the more parents communicated with their kids about sex, the less likely the kids were to have sexual intercourse.[4]

Q: What in your experience confirms these findings?

Q: What in your experience seems to contradict these findings?

Q: What emotions do these findings stir in you?

FYI: If you want to include more research in your presentation, or point your parents to additional online resources, you might want to check out www.4parents.gov. As part of the Parents Speak Up initiative from the U.S. Department of Health and Human Services, the Web site doesn't integrate Scripture or theology, but it's full of practical ideas and tips for parents who want to talk to their kids about sex.

2. YOUR KIDS ARE MORE SEXUALLY ACTIVE THAN YOU THINK. Explain: **Now for the not-so-good news: the average parent far underestimates**

2. 2004 National Campaign to Prevent Teen Pregnancy, "Parents and Teen Pregnancy: What Surveys Show" (Washington DC), http://www.thenationalcampaign.org/national-data/pdf/Parentspollingfactoids2004.pdf (accessed July 27, 2008).

3. Peter S. Bearman and Hanna Bruckner, "Promising the Future: Virginity Pledges and First Intercourse," *American Journal of Sociology* 106, No. 4 (January, 2001): pp. 859–912.

4. Melina M. Bersamin, Samantha Walker, Deborah A. Fisher, and Joel W. Grube, "Correlates of Oral Sex and Vaginal Intercourse in Early and Middle Adolescence," *Journal of Research on Adolescence*, 16, no. 1 (March 2006): pp. 59–68.

the sexual activities of his or her teenager. In a nonscientific study that compared 100 New York teenagers' actual sexual experiences with 100 New York parents' perceptions of their teenagers' sexual experiences, the following gaps emerged:

- 43% of parents said their own teenager had French-kissed. In reality, 84% of students said they had.

- 28% of parents said their own teenager had gotten or given a hickey. In reality, 73% of students said they had.

- 25% of parents said their own teenager had watched an X-rated movie. In reality, 65% of teenagers said they had.

- 10% of parents said their own teenager had received oral sex. In reality, 61% of students said they had.

- 26% of parents said their own teenager had had sexual intercourse. In reality, 55% of students said they had.[5]

Q: Why do you think these gaps exist between parents' perceptions and students' own experiences?

Explain: **Of course, it's possible that students were over-reporting their levels of sexual activity to some degree. But even if that's the case, there's always the possibility that we as parents are a bit naïve—or maybe just overly optimistic—about our kids' sexual choices.**

3. RELIGIOUS PARENTS FIND CONVERSATIONS MORE DIFFICULT, WHICH IS A TRAGIC IRONY. Explain: **Using both the National Study of Youth and Religion telephone survey data and the first wave of the National Longitudinal Study of Adolescent Health survey data, Dr. Mark Regnerus has found that the more important religion is to parents (not just Christianity but also other religions), the more difficult it is for those same parents to talk to their kids about sex.[6]**

5. Stacia Thiel, "Everything You Don't Want to Know About Your Kid's Sex Life," *New York Magazine*, November 12, 2005, http://nymag.com/lifestyle/sex/annual/2005/15078/ (accessed July 27, 2008).

6. Mark Regnerus, *Forbidden Fruit: Sex and Religion in the Lives of American Teenagers* (New York: Oxford University Press, 2007), pp. 60–73.

Q: Why do you think that's the case?

Q: If you wanted to build a case that explained why Christian parents should find it easier to talk to their kids about sex based on what Scripture says, what would you say?

Q: It's been said that it's a "tragic irony" that religious parents find conversations about sex more difficult than less religious parents find them. What do you think about that?

Explain: **Interestingly, Dr. Regnerus also found that mothers are the primary go-to parent for sexual information, especially for daughters.**

Q: Why do you think it works out that way?

Q: What's good about that tendency? What's not so good about it?

Overcome Your Kids' Obstacles by Connecting...

At this point return to the list of obstacles that parents created at the start of the meeting and cross out those that can be overcome by the previous three ideas.

Explain: **Now we're going to talk about how to overcome many of our kids' obstacles. There are two ways to connect with kids: (1) as opportunities arise, and (2) through special rituals.**

1. AS OPPORTUNITIES ARISE Explain: **Just about every day we have opportunities to overcome our kids' obstacles to talking about sex. After all, sex isn't something kids think about periodically; it's something they marinate in 24/7 (literally through their hormones, as well as metaphorically in the media and the subcultures in which they live). Here are some good ideas from other parents that can help you create space for healthy conversations with kids.**

Start with "Them," Not Me

Explain: **Many of the parents who are best at talking with their kids about sex do NOT start by asking about what's happening in their kids' lives. Instead, they take advantage of any external conversation starters that pop up, such as:**

...the girl at school who just announced she was pregnant

...a provocative scene from a movie or TV show

...a news event that involves sex

Maybe the conversation will eventually get more personal, maybe not. Either way, every conversation you have about sex—even if it's about someone else's sexual experiences—makes it a bit easier to have the next one.

Listen, Don't Lecture

Explain: **It's the rare teenager who looks forward to talking to his or her parents about sex.**

Q: Why do you think that is? What is it that students seem to expect their parents to say?

Q: In what tone of voice or with what emotion do they expect us to say those words?

Explain: **Parents who are best at talking to their kids about sex will bite their tongues—sometimes literally—when they feel tempted to lecture their kids. Since the reality is that your kids probably already have a hunch about what you might say about sex, do your best to let** *them* **do the talking.**

Ask, Don't Judge

Explain: **Most teenagers won't launch into a monologue about sex, so if we're going to help them do the talking, then we'll have to ask questions. And we must also do our best to avoid the What-Are-You-Thinking-You-Must-Be-Crazy! tone of voice when we ask them.**

Instead of talking with (or more accurately, *talking at*) your kids, I recommend that you use a strategy that psychiatrists use to deal with teenagers: ask questions. According to Peter Jensen, a former head of child and adolescent research at the National Institutes of Mental Health and current director of the Center for the Advancement of Children's Mental Health, "If you just flat-out tell a teenager what to do, you can lose that kid." Instead, he recommends that parents ask questions to help kids think about the effects of their choices, such as: *What do you think the consequences will be if you act a certain way?* Or *What will happen if you're rejected by your friends when you say you'd rather not look at online pornography?*[7]

Q: In your experience, what types of questions are most effective in drawing out your teenager?

2. THROUGH SPECIAL RITUALS Explain: **When it comes to sexuality, every teenager experiences certain major transitions or milestones. What are some of those milestones?** *(Examples include first menstruation, first date, first boyfriend or girlfriend, first school dance or banquet.)*

Some parents do overnights at hotels or adventure camping trips with their kids ahead of time and let these special events serve as occasions to talk about what their teenager might be experiencing. Others purchase a special gift to commemorate the event. These gifts can be far more creative than just a "purity ring." For example, how about a camera to help a student think about dating with a "new lens," or a chicken neck to demonstrate what you'll do if your kid messes up? (Just kidding.)

Q: In the midst of those milestones, what are some special rituals you've done, or thought about doing, that can mark those occasions for your teenager?

Q: What do these rituals communicate to your teenager about their own sexuality?

Q: What do these rituals communicate to your teenager about *you*?

Explain: **You can choose whether it makes more sense for your kid to experience these rituals with one or both parents. Probably the most important thing is communicating that you understand that these milestones are significant markers in your child's life.**

7. Barbara Strauch, *The Primal Teen: What the New Discoveries about the Teenage Brain Tell Us about Our Kids* (New York: Anchor Books, 2004), pp. 34–35.

HOW (30 minutes)

At this point, ask parents to share various sexual issues or situations that they'd like to talk about with their teenagers. Choose one of these and then invite your parents to get into pairs to practice **How** to apply these tips to a conversation about that issue.

In each pair one parent plays the kid, and other parent plays the parent. Encourage the "kids" to act as they believe their own kids would, while the "parents" try to listen and ask questions.

Circulate around the room, eavesdropping on the pairs' interactions. After a few minutes, stop the pairs and ask:

Q: What's going well in your conversation?

Q: What are your struggles?

Q: What ideas do you have for overcoming these struggles?

Choose a second sexual issue or situation and ask the pairs to reverse roles. After a few minutes, debrief the pairs' interactions by using the same three questions.

Return to the list of obstacles that parents identified at the start of the meeting. Cross off any obstacles that have been addressed already. Then invite the group to brainstorm ways to overcome the remaining obstacles, one at a time. Be honest when an obstacle seems impossible to overcome and encourage parents who face that obstacle to seek additional wisdom through prayer, Scripture study, the advice of other wise parents or a professional counselor, if necessary.

Before you wrap up the meeting, make sure you touch upon the following:

Explain: **Parents are welcome to come to youth group at any time, including when we teach about sex. But when parents come, they need to come with a goal of learning and observing instead of spying on their own kids.**

The African proverb "It takes a village to raise a child" is certainly true when it comes to kids' sexual choices. The more that parents can communicate with you and your team of youth leaders, the better. If appropriate, you might ask parents to suggest ways that your team of adult leaders can communicate helpful information to them (e.g., sharing articles about teenage sexuality, descriptions of the major points discussed in youth group, summaries of the primary Scripture passages studied, and so on).

Close in prayer—either in a large group or in small groups—inviting parents to ask God, the ultimate Parent, to show them how they can best parent their children through the sexual choices they're navigating.

ADDITIONAL IDEAS FOR PARTNERING WITH PARENTS

If we could wave a *Good Sex* Magic Wand for Parents (no, that product is not available for sale from the publisher), we'd love to see you partner with parents in line with three goals:

1. To inform parents about the sexual pressures, thoughts, and feelings bombarding their kids and how students in general (and maybe even their own kids) are holding up under them—including the good news that (as of this writing) teenage abortions are down, teenage pregnancies are down, and teenagers are delaying their first sexual intercourse longer. (That's not the whole story, but it's certainly part of the story.)

2. To involve parents in their kids' sex education, instead of outsourcing it to the school—or to you!

3. To encourage parents as they take steps, even baby steps, in discussing the all-too-often taboo subjects of sex with their own teenagers.

You likely already have some great ideas to help accomplish some of those goals, but perhaps these additional ideas can stir your thinking:

- Schedule a parent meeting and offer snacks (that means real food, not leftover pizza and stale tortilla chips), as well as a safe place to share honestly about why and how parents can have authentic conversations with their kids about sexuality. To that end, we've given you an outline to use with your students' parents on **page 11**.

- Forward valuable tidbits from each lesson to parents, especially lists and provocative comments students make (keeping the students anonymous, of course).

- Send a newsletter to parents to let them know what you're covering when—and how they can be praying.

- Ahead of time, ask a parent you respect to be on call for an extended length of time—six to twelve months—to help other parents navigate through their students' tricky questions or struggles.

- Enlist a team of parents to contact the rest of the parents to ask what your ministry can do to help them.

- Send encouraging stories from anonymous students about how their parents have helped them understand and deal with sex.

- Ask parents to share personal stories during your youth group meetings about how they handled (succeeded, struggled with, failed, recovered, and came to understand) sex when they were teenagers.

- Organize a no holds barred parent panel on marriage and sexuality during which kids get to anonymously ask the questions on index cards. (There's a segment called "Love Stories" on **page 98** in the **Intimacy** session that might open the door to this.)

- Establish a parent advisory board to help all your parents deal with teenage sex and other issues.

- Recommend TV shows, magazines, and Web sites to parents that reflect what their kids deal with sexually. Send parents copies of magazine or online articles (Christian or otherwise), as well as song lyrics, to keep them informed on what their kids deal with sexually.

- Encourage parents to create special rituals to mark significant conversations or decisions their children make about sexual boundaries and self-control. (See **page 17** of the "Parent Meeting" section—the part that mentions rituals—for more on this.)

- Take a case study from each lesson and send it to parents with a few suggested discussion questions they can use with their own kids. (See "Sweet Dreams Are Made of This" on **page 128** or "The King and I" on **page 191** for examples.)

- Suggest that families connect with other families to discuss sexuality. It might actually be easier for kids *and* parents to talk about sex with others around.

Above all, communicate openness and humility (especially if you're young). Parents are *not* your natural enemies, and very few of them are too drug-addled or clueless to engage what's happening with their kids. Most parents will be glad to know you're on the same team.

TALKING POINTS FOR PASTORS AND OTHER BOSSES

There's an old tradition among youth workers that says it's easier to ask forgiveness than permission when dealing with things that people in authority just don't get (but will certainly appreciate after the fact).

You probably know best, but let us just state for the record that, depending on who you are and where you live and what your boss is like, making the unilateral decision to take your group through the *Good Sex* curriculum may not be one of those things.

One of our pastor friends liked our title and decided to borrow it for a series of sermons on the Song of Songs. The church sign—which read GOOD SEX, SUNDAY 9 AND 11—brought a visit from the police who assumed it must be a prank perpetrated by ne'er-do-well kids, because who ever heard of a church using the words *sex* and *good* together? We think it's time to get that perception turned around, if we can. But there's no sense in startling anyone if we can help it.

It may be to everyone's advantage for you to brief your boss on what you're planning, as well as why and how. It may also be worthwhile to show off this handsome Leader's Guide and the Student Journal that goes with it—just so no one is taken by surprise. If the police show up, it's better if everyone has the same story.

If you decide it's wise to brief your head of staff, boss, committee, or whomever, here are a few talking points to help you prepare.

By the way, we've done this before. This is edition 2.0 of the *Good Sex* curriculum, thoroughly revised and updated to take advantage of new research, improved teaching methods, and generous user input from the first edition.

Assessing *Good Sex 1.0* for *Christianity Today*, Tim Stafford wrote:
> Hancock and Powell explain that they aim for a process, not a confrontation. In seven lessons they cover a lot of biblical ground. The Bible studies are bracketed by open-ended discussion, in which kids think for themselves and speak freely. The intent is to create a church context in which sexuality gets explored thoughtfully and biblically, and kids reach their own conclusions.[8]

He got exactly what we were after. For the reasons we explore on **page 8**, the *Good Sex* curriculum is a learner-centered design. You may want to flash that page around a bit so your supervisor understands why you're not standing on a chair telling kids what to think and how to behave—not that you don't have thoroughly biblical ideas about that, but you want to guide kids into discovering and embracing those ideas themselves. You know, the way people actually learn and internalize behavioral choices.

Show off the "Partnering with Parents" page and the "Parent Meeting" plan, too. It's important for the boss to know you're not just doing all this in plain sight, but you also want to include parents as much as they're willing to be included. Point out the "Love Stories" element on **page 98** (where you interview a married couple from your Christian community) and "The Home Front" on **page 207** (where you interview parents in front of your group).

Perhaps most important, make it clear that you'll need support if you bump into a case of abuse or a student with a medical issue or something else unforeseen. Show your boss our advice on **page 259** for what to do if you need a referral for a kid in trouble.

Most bosses—and understand that we use the term loosely, to describe whomever and however many supervise your work—want their youth workers to engage students in things that matter. They just don't want to be surprised by someone who really doesn't get it storming in, demanding answers that your supervisors don't have because they didn't know what you were doing.

---

8. Tim Stafford, "Let's Talk Sex," *Christianity Today*, June 2004, p. 36.

So…use your best judgment.

Kara Powell + Jim Hancock

p.s. If you ARE the boss, we're delighted you've found this greeting.

No offense to anyone else, but that's doubly true if you serve a normal-sized congregation under 200. We have a soft spot in our hearts for solo and bi-vocational pastors who hold the adolescents in their congregations in high regard. Whether you use this resource yourself or put it in the hands of caring laypeople, we really hope you find it adaptable and useful. Let us know what you think…

SESSION 1

SESSION ONE | SEX MESSAGING

For Your Own Preparation

> Suppose you came to a country where you could fill a theatre by simply
> bringing a covered plate on to the stage and then slowly lifting the cover
> so as to let every one see, just before the lights went out, that it contained
> a mutton chop or a bit of bacon, would you not think that in that country
> something had gone wrong with the appetite for food?[9]

C. S. Lewis wrote that in the 1940s. We think he was on to something. We think maybe something has gone wrong with our appetite for sex. Pretty much any way you look at it, our culture is preoccupied with sex way out of proportion to its actual significance.

The kids you serve have grown up largely unprotected from what grown-ups cynically refer to as "adult content." But they didn't introduce all that to the sexual equation, did they?

So how do we help our students understand and enjoy and take responsibility for their sexuality? How do we equip them for life in the world where they live instead of some Neverland where children don't wrestle with sexuality?

Do we throw up our hands or dig in our heels? Do we ignore biblical messages written "too long ago" and "too far away" to be much use in the 21st century? Or alter them to fit modern sensibilities? Or do we hunker down and defend our tiny square of turf until the last of us dies off and the world goes to hell?

9. C. S. Lewis, *Mere Christianity* (New York: Collier Books/Macmillan, 1964), p. 96.

Things are messy. But not messier than what's recorded in the Bible. The earliest Christian communities flourished in cultures where sexual norms were flat-out abusive. Those folks lived in places where sexual slavery was a given; where women and girls were property—collected, traded, used, and discarded. They lived in cities where boys were sex objects for wealthy men. And no one raised an eyebrow, let alone a helping hand.

People who loved Jesus stood out in those cultures. And it wasn't so much what they said as the way they lived. God's people reinvented the family by living in committed marriage, instilling respect for women, and protecting and nurturing children instead of exploiting them.

> You never change anything by fighting it; you change things by making them obsolete through superior technology.
> — Buckminster Fuller
>
> Mike Vance and Diane Deacon, *Think Out of the Box* (Franklin Lakes, NJ: Career Press, 1997), p. 138.

These ideas were huge, not because smart people wrote about them but because ordinary people lived them out.

That's what we're after here: To contrast the sexual messages that kids grow up hearing and seeing with the much more optimistic view of sexuality in the biblical tradition. Somehow, what we call "the Church" has lost the thread of sexual wholeness along with everybody else. Maybe it's time to stop obsessing about the sexual norms that surround us and steadily but quietly help kids grow into their sexuality healthy and whole.

This session explores the messages that students routinely receive about sex and invites them to begin engaging the biblical text as a source of information and guidance about who they are as whole people—including their sexuality.

Reflect for a Moment

We can't lead students where we're not willing to go ourselves. We can point them… but they'd rather be guided. Here are a few questions to consider as you prepare to lead this session on sex messaging.

Q: If a totally objective stranger had absolute access to your life, where do you think she'd say you got your ideas about sex?

• What influences do you think she'd say were healthy for you?

• What influences do you think she'd say were unhealthy?

Q: Forget about the totally objective stranger: what do you wish you'd learned sooner?

• Is there anything you wish you could go back and *unlearn*?

Q: If you had just one hour to talk with kids about sex, what would you try to communicate?

• Why do you think that's so important?

• If you couldn't lecture on the subject, how would you try to communicate during that hour?

NOW | Where Did You Learn about Sex? (10 minutes)

The Big Idea: Some of the ways we learn about sexuality are more trustworthy than others.

Play the video, then ask—

Q: What's the truest thing you heard in that piece? Why do you think that's true?

Q: Were any sources of sexual information missing from the video?

Distribute the *Where Did You Learn about Sex?* handout and talk through the questions together.

Here's a quote you can use in the discussion if you wish:

> The debate over whether to have sex education in American schools is over. A new poll by NPR, the Kaiser Family Foundation, and Harvard's Kennedy School of Government finds that only 7 percent of Americans say sex education should not be taught in schools… However, this does not mean that all Americans agree on what kind of sex education is best. There are major differences over the issue of abstinence. Fifteen percent of Americans believe that schools should teach only about abstinence from sexual intercourse and should not provide information on how to obtain and use condoms and other contraception. A plurality (46 percent) believes that the most appropriate approach is one that might be called "abstinence-plus"—that while abstinence is best, some teens do not abstain, so schools also should teach about condoms and contraception. Thirty-six percent believe that abstinence is not the most important thing, and that sex ed should focus on teaching teens how to make responsible decisions about sex.
>
> NPR/Kaiser/Kennedy School Poll, "Sex Education in America," February 24, 2004, http://www.npr.org/templates/story/story.php?storyId=1622610 (accessed July 27, 2008).

You'll need—
• A television or video projection unit
• DVD player
• The *Good Sex* DVD, cued to "Where Did You Learn about Sex?"
• Copies of *Where Did You Learn about Sex?* handout (on DVD) or Student Journal (**page 12**)
• Pencils

Instead of playing the DVD, with a little preparation, you can have students perform "Where Did You Learn about Sex?" The video transcript is on the DVD.

FYI: If the writer Michael Gurian is right, by age 18, American teenagers have seen approximately 100,000 sex acts in the visual media.

Michael Gurian, "The Church Is Failing Sex Ed," *U.S. Catholic* 6, no. 3 (March 2000), pp. 26–30.

Transition: **Let's explore Mark 10 as a next step in our discussion about sexuality.**

NEW | Male + Female | Bible Study (20 minutes)

The Big Idea: Any serious discussion of sexuality begins with the truth that men and women are both created in God's image.

You'll need—
- Bibles
- Copies of the *Soft Hearts* handout (on DVD) or Student Journal (**page 16**)
- Pencils

FYI: In Jesus' day, the rabbinic teachings on divorce established a double standard for men and women. It was taught that an unfaithful wife was committing adultery against *her husband* while an unfaithful husband who had sex with another man's wife had committed adultery against *that woman's husband* (not his own wife). In contrast, Jesus levels the playing field and says in Mark 10:11 that an unfaithful husband commits adultery against *his own wife*.

Explain: **You can't believe everything you hear. I know that doesn't come as a shock to you. Jesus underscored this when some religious leaders approached him about sexual relationships. It's in Mark 10:1-12...**

Read Mark 10:1-12 together, then ask—

Q: What point do you think Jesus was making in his response to these religious leaders?

Q: Does anyone recognize the biblical passages Jesus quotes here: "God 'made them male and female'" and "'For this reason a man will leave his father and mother and be united to his wife, and the two will become one flesh'"?

Explain: **The first quotation is from Genesis 1:27—**
So God created human beings in his own image,
in the image of God he created them;
male and female he created them.

The second quotation is from Genesis 2:24—
For this reason a man will leave his father and mother and be united to his wife, and they will become one flesh.

The religious leaders challenged Jesus with the law of Moses on divorce. Jesus responded by going back to the first principles in creation:
1. Men and women are both created in God's image.
2. The union of a woman and a man in marriage is not a disposable relationship.

You may be wondering why either idea was ever in question. William Barclay says the problem Jesus was addressing hinged on the fact that,

In Jewish law a woman was regarded as a thing. She had no legal rights whatever but was at the complete disposal of the male head of the family. The result was that a man could divorce his wife on almost any grounds, while there were very few on which a woman could seek divorce. At best she could only ask her husband to divorce her. "A woman may be divorced with or without her will, but a man only with his will."[10]

So...you can see the problem: In Matthew's telling of the story (Matthew 19:1-11), the religious leaders asked, "Is it lawful for a man to divorce his wife for any and every reason?" (verse 3). The people with unlimited power wanted even more power to do exactly as they pleased. I doubt that comes as a shock to you either.

Q: Do you have a theory about why people with power sometimes try to grab even more power?

• How have you seen that played out between people who claim to love each other?

Q: Is there anyone here who hasn't seen that kind of selfishness damage a relationship?

• If you've seen self-seeking power ruin a relationship, then—without revealing the identity of the people you're talking about—can you tell us what you saw?

Q: Glance back through Mark 10:1-12 to answer this question: Do you think Jesus implies a solution to the problem of selfishness between husbands and wives? Talk about that.

Explain: **If I was going to pick a clue from what Jesus says here, then I think I would call it "soft hearts." Jesus said, "It was because your hearts were *hard* that Moses wrote you this law" (Mark 10:5, emphasis added). Soft hearts...**

Distribute the *Soft Hearts* handout and talk through the questions together.

FYI: In the very next beat (Mark 10:13-15), Jesus gives an equally countercultural answer to the question, *Are adults worth more than children?* It doesn't take much imagination to see how the words and actions of Jesus call us to reassess the value we place on culturally powerful and powerless people.

---

10. William Barclay, *The Gospel of Mark: The New Daily Study Bible*. (Louisville, KY: Westminster John Knox Press, 2001), p. 276.

When you complete the handout…

Explain: **You might think this would go without saying, but maybe any serious conversation about sexuality has to begin with the questions:** *Are women better than men?* **and** *Are men better than women?*

Q: Based on what we've read in Mark 10:1-12, what answer does Jesus give?

Q: If someone asked you to identify the point of this discussion, what would you say?

Transition: **You know the old saying, "It takes a village to raise a kid"? Well, some of the members of that village are other kids. I'm convinced you need each other and can be there for each other. I want us to spend the rest of this session thinking about ways we can help each other understand and grow in our sexuality.**

HOW | SexTalk: Sex Messaging **(20 minutes)**

The Big Idea: Maybe it's time for Christians to stop obsessing over other people's sex lives and quietly help each other grow into our own sexuality healthy and whole.

Play the DVD, then ask—

Q: What idea or phrase stuck with you from that piece?

Q: Why do you think that's significant?

Read Mark 12:28-34 together.

Explain: **The word that's translated into English here as all—*all* your heart, *all* your soul, *all* your mind, *all* your strength—is a peculiar word that carries the meaning of "everything," "the sum total," "the whole enchilada," "ALL." I'm just joking around. *All* means "all." That's all it can mean.**

Let's make a quick list of human traits and experiences included in all your heart, all your soul, all your mind, and all your strength. You call them out, and I'll write them down.

Q: Do you have any reason to think your sexuality is not part of *all your heart, all your soul, all your mind, and all your strength*?

> You'll need—
> • A television or video projection unit
> • DVD player
> • The *Good Sex* DVD, cued to "SexTalk: Sex Messaging"
> • List-making supplies
> • Copies of the *Can I Be Perfectly Honest with You?* handout (on DVD) or Student Journal (**page 18**)
>
> If you have a talented actor or reader in your group, he or she could read "SexTalk: Sex Messaging" instead of you playing the DVD. The video transcript is on the DVD.

Explain: **In this series of sessions called *Good Sex*, we're going to explore deeply what it means to love God with ALL, including our sexuality.**

We'll also explore what it means to keep the second most important commandment: "Love your neighbor as yourself." I think that begins with agreeing on how safe we want this room to be. So, let's talk for a moment about making this group a safe place to talk about sexuality.

Distribute the handout *Can I Be Perfectly Honest with You?* and go through it together.

When you reach the end of the handout, ask:

Q: Does that seem fair?

Continue: **If it does, I'd like each of us to say it out loud to everyone else. I'll go first, and then I'm going to ask someone else if he or she is willing to join me in this commitment. If so, then that person will make the commitment and then ask someone else to join him or her.**

Anyone who's uncomfortable making the commitment can just say, "I need to think about it some more," or "I pass."

Okay, first me: "I'll keep what we say here confidential unless someone's life is in danger, and I'm asking you to do the same thing."

(Ask someone else to make the commitment, then prompt the process until everyone has agreed or taken a pass. Of course you'll need to follow up with anyone who's not comfortable promising to keep the confidence of the others in the group.)

Continue: **One last thing. At the end of the video clip, he talked about quietly helping each other grow into our own sexuality healthy and whole.**

Q: What do you think it would take for us to develop that kind of Christian community?
• What do you think we might need to start doing?
• What do you think we might need to stop doing?
• Where do you think we might get what it takes to do that for each other?

Conclude: Lead the group in a prayer of thanksgiving for our sexuality and hope that God will enable your group to grow into the kind of generous people who'll never take advantage of anyone's weakness and always help each grow up healthy and whole.

Other Resources for Teaching on Sex Messaging

NOW | Where in the World Are You? (15 minutes)

The Big Idea: Where we stand and where we'd like to go together

Explain: **Hopefully, this group can be a safe place for us to discuss the sexual messages and pressures that bombard us all the time. And, hopefully, we'll figure out what God would say back to us through the Bible and through each other.**

We don't want to waste anybody's time here—not yours, nor mine. To make sure we all understand the most important questions and issues we're facing, I'd like to give you time to complete this *Where in the World Are You?* handout and give it back to me.

I'm not going to do a handwriting analysis or anything to try to figure out who wrote what. It's completely anonymous, so I hope you'll feel free to identify where you're at now, as well as where you'd like to be.

Distribute the *Where in the World Are You?* handout and give students enough time to answer the questions.

After students complete their handouts, if you wish, put them in groups of three or four and ask them to share one or two things they wrote. After a few minutes, reconvene the session and ask:

You'll need—
• Copies of the *Where in the World Are You?* handout (on DVD) or Student Journal (**page 19**)
• Pencils

FYI: You may want to do this as part of a group session, or you may want to distribute it to be completed and returned apart from a group session.

In any event, take time to understand the feedback you get. It will help you set the direction for your teaching on sexuality. It may also be a wake-up call for parents and other adults around you.

Q: What did you hear from your friends just now that rings true with you?

Q: Would you say you more welcome or dread the idea of discussing sexuality in our group? Why is that?

Q: If you could get me to hear one important thing on this subject, what would that be?

Conclude this element by asking God to give each person the wisdom to help each other understand and enjoy our sexuality under the lordship of Jesus.

NOW | *Loveline* | Discussion (15 minutes)

The Big Idea: Assessing the sorts of questions and answers kids hear about sex

Ask—

Q: How many of you have heard of the show *Loveline*? *(Pick one or two people who raise their hands.)* Describe it for us briefly.

If no one raises a hand, say: ***Loveline* is a radio call-in show where people ask the hosts and various celebrity guests questions about sex.**

Distribute the *Loveline* handout and work through the first caller together.

When you finish discussing the first caller...

Explain: **The *Loveline* hosts told Adam to stay out of the situation because he has absolutely nothing to offer this child. It's better if the child never knows who his father is.** *(And, no, if anyone asks, the first caller was not longtime* Loveline *cohost Adam Carolla.)*

Return to the handout and work through the second caller together.

When you finish discussing the second caller...

Explain: **The *Loveline* hosts told Toni to stay out of it and let the couple work it out themselves.**

Return to the handout and work through the third caller together.

When you finish discussing the third caller...

You'll need—
• A television or video projection unit
• DVD player
• Copies of the *Loveline* handout (on DVD) or Student Journal (**page 23**)
• Pencils

FYI: *Loveline* is a nationally syndicated radio show (still on the air and streaming on the Web at this writing) originating from Southern California. Callers check in from across the nation to talk about sexual issues with Dr. Drew Pinsky and his cohost and guests. Questions and answers on *Loveline* are pretty much no holds barred, so if you ever tune in, be forewarned. That said, *Loveline* is readily available to any kid with a radio or an Internet connection, so...

FYI: If *Loveline* becomes irrelevant or goes off the air before you use this session, just say: **Back in the day, there was a radio show called *Loveline*—ever hear of it?** And go on from there.

Explain: **The *Loveline* hosts told Melissa she had a compulsive addiction to sex that had been triggered by this event. She was told to get counseling and hook up with an AA-type group.**

Q: Given the advice that the *Loveline* hosts gave that night, how likely would you be to suggest that a friend call in to try to talk to them about a sexual issue?

FYI: We're not recommending *Loveline*. We're acknowledging that it's there and accessible on free radio and Internet for anyone to hear and that it can be disturbing and glib and crude, as well as honest, compassionate, and helpful. If that's a problem for you, skip it and move on (as if you needed our permission...).

Explain: **Sometimes the hosts on *Loveline* give straightforward and generally compassionate advice. Other times, not so much... I wonder if folks—even Christian folks—turn to *Loveline* because they believe that most churches and Christians are too scared (or judgmental) to talk about sex as directly and honestly as they do on *Loveline*.**

Q. Do you agree that most churches and Christians don't talk about sex in a direct and honest way? Talk about that...

NOW | Commercial Breaks | Video + Discussion (10 minutes)

The Big Idea: Assessing the messages kids hear about sex on television

In Advance: record a half-dozen afternoon or nighttime commercials from CNN, MSNBC, or Fox News and a half-dozen afternoon or nighttime commercials from MTV or Comedy Central.

Identify the sources and play your recording for the group. Then ask—

Q: How did those messages attempt to employ sexuality as a motivator?

• How successful do you think they were?

• Did you notice any difference between the newsy shows and the entertainment shows? Talk about that.

Q: Beyond successful or unsuccessful selling, how true-to-life is their use of sexuality?

Q: What do these messages suggest about how the sellers see their customers?

• How close is that to the way you see yourself and your peers?

Q: Companies use these advertising messages because they believe they sell products. What are your thoughts on that?

• If you could give advertisers one message about sexual content, what would you say?

NOW | RU Sexualized? | Discussion (15 minutes)

The Big Idea: Girls are especially at risk to being over-sexualized in our culture.

Explain: **In 2007, the American Psychological Association Task Force on the Sexualization of Girls issued a report on the troubling objectification of girls. Here is a passage from the executive summary of that report.**

You'll need—
• Copies of the *RU Sexualized?* handout (on DVD) or Student Journal (**page 25**)
• Pencils

Distribute the *RU Sexualized?* handout and talk through it together.

When you reach the end of the handout...

For more on this report, turn to **page 69**.

Conclude this element by asking God to give every young woman and man in the room the wisdom to view and understand themselves as a whole person, created in God's image and never, ever a sexual object. Ask God for resilience to bounce back from experiences of sexualization, no matter what the source, and the strength to resist sexualizing or being sexualized in the future.

HOW | Shred | Discussion (10 minutes)

The Big Idea: Each one of us has a sexual identity.

Keeping the shredder hidden, distribute sheets of paper and something to write with. Then invite the group to write negative and sexualizing messages they've encountered anywhere and at any time in their lives—about themselves or anyone else. As they finish writing, ask them to stack their sheets together. Then read some of them out loud.

> You'll need—
> • Paper
> • Pencils or markers
> • Paper shredder
> • Trash can or bags

Ask—

Q: Can you talk about any of these messages that you've taken to heart in a way that damaged your sense of who you are as a person created in God's image?

• How do you feel about that now?

Explain: **God loves us just the way we are—and far too much to leave us that way. I'm going to give you an opportunity to do something symbolic that celebrates God's mercy and goodness.**

Spread the sheets out on the floor or table with the negative messages showing. Invite each student to choose a message that has significance for him or her (or to create alternates if they don't see messages that express what they're feeling or thinking at the moment).

Bring out the paper shredder and offer a prayer of hope and gratitude for God's mercy and goodness in all things—especially the difficult things in life. Then invite people to approach the shredder—one at a time—and destroy the sheet(s) they have in their hands.

At some point either during or at the end of the procession to the shredder, read 1 John 1:8–2:6 out loud.

Ask—

Q: How does it feel to destroy negative messages about who you are?

• What message would you like to speak to replace that message?

Q: What message do you think God would like to give to you to replace that message?

• Do you think that's all there is to it? What can we do to help you replace that old, false message with a fresh, true one?

Conclude this element by inviting everyone to join hands and talk out loud to God about ignoring false sexual messages and believing true messages.

SESSION 2

SESSION TWO | SEXUAL IDENTITY

For Your Own Preparation

The first pages of the first book of the Bible say God made humans male and female. Women and men are a matched set. Both are necessary for reproduction; each benefits from the uniqueness of the other. That's sex; that's gender. Two X chromosomes deliver a female; an X and a Y produce a male. Different body chemistry, different physical structures—it's not rocket science.

Sexual identity is a different matter. Sexual identity is how we experience our sexuality, and what we think and how we feel about that. And then what we do about it. This has a lot to do with hormones—testosterone in boys and progesterone in girls. But it also has something to do with how we're treated by our families, friends, schools, mass media—the whole culture. That's what this session is mainly about.

Kids' families and friends and communities influence how they think about their sexuality from the day they're born. Women and men tell boys and girls how to act; kids watch adults and learn how it's really done. And they read, listen to the radio, go to the playground, and watch TV shows and movies. Bit by bit they come to understand themselves as males and females, which determines, for the most part, how they play and dress and talk and relate to other people.

All is well in the neighborhood. Until puberty hits like a flash flood, and kids are up to their hips in hormones and high waters.

Chubby boys grow angular; their voices crack and drop; muscles mass and occasionally cramp in places where there didn't even used to *be* places; hair sprouts like patches of grass; unanticipated erections ambush them by day, and erotic dreams produce involuntary ejaculations of semen by night. It is, without question, a crazy time of life.

Skinny girls find their straight lines replaced by curving hips and bellies; their breasts bud and grow (evenly, they hope); they experience unexpected attention from much older males; new hair grows on them, too—although generally not as densely as on their brothers; and they cross their fingers, hoping against the odds that they'll be safe at home when they get their first period. These are exceedingly strange days for girls morphing into women.

Some kids seem utterly unselfconscious about their sexuality; others are conspicuously self-aware.

In the locker room, one boy saunters to the shower wearing nothing but a smile and a towel around his neck. The boy at the next locker wraps his towel around his waist like a kilt and holds it carefully lest he fall prey to a towel snatcher roaming the aisles of metal lockers. On the way they pass a kid who doesn't need a towel because there's no way he's going near the shower.

In the classroom a girl, dressed for comfort, is oblivious to the boy who sits behind her, transfixed by the curve of her bare shoulder. The girl in front of her is dressed to get attention and seems fully aware of her effect on boys: "She ain't got much," another girl whispers to her friend, "but it's all out there where they can get a look at it." At the back of the room, for reasons that are private and painful, another girl wears baggy clothes to hide her sexuality.

And so it goes in adolescence; the unconscious and the hyperconscious, questioning, defining, and redefining their sexual identity.

What do kids want to know about their sexual identity?

Well…ask around to be sure, but here's a short list of things that kids everywhere seem to wonder:
- Am I normal?
- Are my sexual responses normal?
- Why do I get nervous around people of the other gender?
- Why do I get turned on so easily?
- Do I get turned on like other people?
- Why do I feel guilty about my sexuality?

- Am I a sex fiend?
- Am I gay?
- Could I turn gay?

This list hasn't changed much in the last 50 years. Curiosity about homosexuality may have escalated a bit—kids generally talk about homosexuality more comfortably than their parents did back in the day. Other than that, the list looks about the same.

In the midst of kids' questions, Christians who sit down for reasonable, biblically informed conversations about sexuality are few and far between. Half the Church gets laryngitis when kids ask about these things. The other half shouts louder.

One of our dirty little secrets is that Christians don't always agree on the subject of sexuality.

Take gender roles, for instance.

Some Christians believe there are male jobs (thinking, heavy lifting, bringing home the bacon) and female jobs (cooking the bacon, cleaning, bearing and raising children) because that's the way God likes it. Anybody who crosses the behavioral divide has some explaining to do.

Other Christians believe the only differences between men and women are cultural and therefore nonbiblical, if not frankly *un*biblical.

People in these two camps have been known to wonder if those in the other camp are even Christians.

Or take homosexuality:
- Some Christians think homosexuality is a perversion, plain and simple (like sacrificing babies to Molech).
- Some think homosexuality is a complex sin (like alcohol dependency).
- Some think homosexuality is a biological abnormality (like a mutant gene).
- Some think homosexuality is a normal genetic trait (like blond hair).
- Some think homosexuality is a lifestyle choice (like voting Republican).

Jam all those opinions into one room, and things get pretty noisy. Or very quiet. For a lot of Christians, it's easier to not have the conversation at all.

That's a mistake. Maybe this goes without saying, but if we don't address kids' questions about sexual identity, someone else will. In fact, someone else already *is*—loud and late into the night.

So we'd better.

Creating a Safe Environment for Teaching About Sexual Identity...

- Don't make jokes about sexual identity in public or private.
- Don't listen to jokes about sexual identity in public or private.
- Don't put up with jokes about sexual identity in your youth group.
- Resolve your own sexual identity and behavioral choices—get help where necessary to complete unfinished business.
- Take it *very* seriously when a student is willing to talk with you about sexual identity issues. Self-identified bisexual and homosexual adolescents and those who have same-sex sexual encounters or report same-sex romantic attraction or relationships are at greater risk of:
  - o Assault—45 percent of homosexual men and 20 percent of homosexual women report being verbally or physically assaulted in high school, specifically because of their sexual orientation.
  - o Dropping out of school, being kicked out of home, and living on the street
  - o Frequent and heavy use of tobacco, alcohol, marijuana, cocaine, and other drugs at an earlier age
  - o Sexual intercourse, multiple partners, and rape
  - o Sexually transmitted diseases, including HIV
  - o Suicide—they're anywhere from twice as likely to seven times as likely to attempt suicide as self-identified heterosexual classmates.
  - o The data doesn't link these risk factors to sexual identity *per se*, but they're conspicuously coupled with negative reactions to gender nonconformity, stress, violence, lack of support, family problems, peer suicides, and homelessness.

- Don't use the Bible selectively to make a point or back people into a corner—it's not that kind of sword.
- Make it clear that you're open to talking with any student about any issue of sexual behavior or sexual identity in a respectful, honest, and open way.
- Don't draw distinctions between heterosexual, homosexual, and bisexual lust. Lust isn't permissible no matter what your sexual identity and theology is. The implication that your lust is somehow better than your neighbor's is just ridiculous.
- Draw clear distinctions between sexual experiences and sexual identity. Many children experience various levels of same-sex preadolescent sex play with other children. Later, most see such experiences as child's play. A few attach more significance to those experiences in retrospect and need the assurance

that it's a fairly common experience of growing up. The introduction of a much older child, adolescent, or adult to the story changes an experience of child's play into a sexually abusive encounter. Some victims of childhood or early adolescent sexual abuse come to believe they may be homosexual because they participated in same-sex activities, or bisexual because they had sexualized encounters with people of both genders.

- Know this: You don't get to vote on a student's sexual attitudes, beliefs, and behaviors any more than she gets to vote on yours. You can listen, learn, advise, teach, seek to understand, and persuade; but you can't control. Nobody can. Apart from killing your young friend outright, your influence over her sexual identity and choices is limited by your humanity. So if you can help it, don't slam doors (other than those that protect other young people). As long as you're still talking, there's hope for a positive outcome.[11]

11. Adapted from Rich Van Pelt and Jim Hancock, *The Youth Worker's Guide to Helping Teenagers in Crisis* (Grand Rapids, Mich.: YS/Zondervan, 2005), pp. 194–195.

Reflect for a Moment

We can't lead students where we're not willing to go ourselves. We can point them... but they'd rather be guided. Here are a few questions to consider as you prepare to lead this session on sexual identity.

Think about your own sexual identity when you were eight years old.

Q: What did you think it meant to be a woman?

Q: What did you think it meant to be a man?

Fast-forward to age 15.

Q: How did your ideas about manhood change from childhood? What do you think influenced those changes?

Q: How did your ideas about womanhood change from childhood? What do you think influenced those changes?

Fast-forward to the present.

Q: List the most important components of authentic masculinity. How did you reach your conclusions?

Q: List the most important components of authentic femininity. How did you reach those conclusions?

Q: Are there things that as a child you believed about your sexual identity that you no longer believe today? Spend some time thinking, writing, or talking with someone about that.

Q: Do you have unanswered questions about sexual identity? Spend some time thinking, writing, or talking with someone about that.

Q: If you had just one hour to talk with kids about sexual identity, what would you try to communicate?

• Why do you think that's so important?

• If you were prevented from lecturing on the subject, how would you try to communicate during that hour?

NOW | SexID (15 minutes)

The Big Idea: Each one of us has a sexual identity.

Play the video, then ask—

Q: What image or phrase stands out from the video?

Q: Why do you think that's important?

Q: Do you identify with someone in the video? Talk about that.

Q: Did anything in the video seem shocking to you?

At this point pull out your driver's license and perhaps encourage your students who have their licenses to get theirs out also. (Be prepared to have your own driver's license picture mocked.)

Explain: **Like most I.D. cards, a driver's license describes aspects of who you are. In the case of the driver's license, it describes your physical identity or what you look like.**

Continue: **The stories we just saw in the video show us a different sort of identity: sexual identity. Our sexual identities are made up of our thoughts, feelings, and attitudes about our sexuality. Just like other facets of your identity as a teenager are in the process of being formed, so is your sexual identity.**

Q: Imagine that the people we saw on the video had not just driver's licenses, but also "Sex I.D." cards. What do you think would be on the cards?

Distribute copies of the *SexID* handout (on DVD) or have students turn to **page 31** of the Student Journal for a chance to think about their own sexual identities. After giving them some time to write about or discuss the questions on the handout, lead the following discussion:

You'll need—
- A television or video projection unit
- DVD player
- The *Good Sex* DVD, cued to "SexID"
- Copies of the *SexID* handout (on DVD) or Student Journal (**page 31**)
- Pencils
- Your driver's license

Instead of playing the DVD, with a little preparation, you can have students perform "SexID." The video transcript is on the DVD.

Q: How would you define *sexual identity*?

Q: In what ways do you think your sexual identity is still in the process of being shaped?

Q: Based on the video, as well as your own experiences, what forces seem to shape our sexual identities?

Q: The video ends with the question, "Why do we do this to each other?" What is "this"?

• What is your answer to the question?

Transition to the next step by explaining: **The handout asked you to describe the role that you'd like God to play in your sexual identity. But how do you think God answers that question? What role does God want to play in how you think, feel, and act sexually? Today we're going to reflect and talk about that together.**

STEP 3: HOW

STEP 2:
NEW

STEP 1

NEW

MON

NEW | Storytime (25 minutes)

The Big Idea: We find our ultimate identity when we find ourselves in God's Story.

Explain: **Understanding and embracing God's role in our sexual identities begins with understanding God's role in our lives overall.**

In *Sex God*, Rob Bell tells a story that's helped me think more deeply about both my sexual identity and God's role in my life. Rob writes:

> When I was five, my family visited my grandparents in California during Christmas vacation. They lived in an apartment building with an alley beside it—very exciting for a boy who lived on a farm in Michigan. At some point in my exploration of the alley, I decided to make a Christmas present for my dad out of the things I had found there. So on the morning of the twenty-fifth, my father had the privilege of opening a gift of a piece of black and green drainpipe glued to a flat gray rock with little white stones resting on the inside of it.

> A masterpiece, to say the least.

> The reason I remember this is because I visited my dad at his office a few days ago, and while I waited for him to finish his meeting, I wandered around looking at the pictures on his walls and the papers on his desk and the things on his shelves. On one of his shelves sat the drainpipe and rock sculpture, thirty years later.

> He still has it.

> He brought it home with him and put it in his office in 1977 and hasn't gotten rid of it.[12]

You'll need—
- Four pieces of poster paper, hung next to each other
- Pens
- Bibles
- In advance meet with four students so they can help you explain the four movements of God's Story.

Q: Why do you think Rob's dad kept the drainpipe-and-rock sculpture for 30 years?

---

12. Rob Bell, *Sex God* (Grand Rapids, Mich: Zondervan, 2007), p. 27.

Q: Sometimes we feel like no more than what's left over from an apartment alley. You might be feeling like you don't have much more value than a bunch of pipes and rocks glued together by a five-year-old. Imagine the dad in the office is actually your heavenly Father. Imagine him looking at you—the drainpipe-and-rock sculpture—sitting on his shelf. What expression is on God's face as God looks at you?

At this point ask your first student volunteer to explain: **Rob's story reminds me of another story—the story of God's interactions with humans throughout history. God's story starts just like Rob's; in Genesis 1:26-27, we learn that we were created special, that we were created in God's image, which means we were created Good.**

> FYI: The "glory" that we've fallen short of in Romans 3:23 seems to refer to the majesty of God's holiness and... well...God's God-ness.

At this point, your first student volunteer should read Genesis 1:26-27 and write the word *Good* in large letters at the top of the first sheet of poster paper.

Have the second volunteer explain the next movement of the story: **Now comes the bad news. Our inherent goodness from being created in God's image has been marred by what happened in the garden of Eden. Every single person on this planet has been tainted by Guilt because of our sin.**

At this point your second student volunteer should read Romans 3:23 and Romans 6:23 and write the word *Guilt* in large letters at the top of the second sheet of poster paper.

Have your third volunteer come up to the third sheet of poster paper, write the word *Grace* in large letters at the top, and then sit down. Give students some time to sit in silence, staring at the word. After at least 60 seconds, ask the third student to come back to where she's written the word *Grace* and lead this discussion:

Q: When you think of grace, what images or phrases come to your mind?

> Whether you believe that image [of God] was obliterated or merely obstructed, the end result is roughly the same: Our world and relationships are broken. Because of our universal sin, every single one of us—from the richest investor on Wall Street to the nameless child caught up in sex trafficking on the streets of Calcutta—is broken.
>
> Chap Clark and Kara E. Powell, *Deep Justice in a Broken World* (Grand Rapids, Mich.: YS/Zondervan, 2008), p. 44.

Q: Given what we've heard about the way we're created as Good and then experience Guilt because of our sin, how should that affect the way we respond to the Grace that God offers?

Note: If none of your students mention that it's because of Jesus' life, death, and resurrection that we're able to embrace God's grace, then please make sure that you do.

At this point, the fourth volunteer should come up to the fourth piece of poster paper, write the word *Gratitude*, and explain: **The Grace that God offers us prompts us to want to serve God out of Gratitude for all that God has done for us. Our lives become great big thank-you notes back to God.**

Ideally, this student would read aloud Ephesians 2:8-10 and then affirm a few ways that kids in your youth ministry are already living their lives as thank-you notes back to God.

At this point help students connect the Good/Guilt/Grace/Gratitude story to their sexual identities by moving to the first piece of poster paper and asking: **How does the first part of this story, which tells us we were created as good and in God's image, relate to our sexual identities?** Make sure to jot down their answers on the poster paper. (As a side note, you might also encourage your students to consider how the fact that others are likewise created in God's image affects how they relate to them sexually.)

Move to the second sheet of poster paper and ask: **How has Guilt—both our own sin and the sins that others have done to us—affected our sexual identities?**

FYI: Students who read the Bible more frequently and say they try to do what the Bible says report fewer instances of sex.

Mark Regnerus, *Forbidden Fruit* (New York: Oxford University Press, 2007), p. 134.

Head to the third poster paper and ask: **In 2 Corinthians 5:17, Paul writes, "Therefore, if anyone is in Christ, the new creation has come: The old has gone, the new is here!" How does the Grace that makes us a new creation relate to our sexual identities?**

You guessed it—stroll on over to the fourth piece of poster paper and ask: **What would it look like to live our sexual identities as thank-you notes back to God?**

You might want to point out some research that highlights the impact of grounding our identity in our faith. The more devoted teenagers are to their religion…

- the greater their belief that they should wait for marriage to have sex.
- the lower their belief that it's okay for teenagers to have sex if they're emotionally ready.
- the less likely they are to have seen pornographic movies, Web sites, or videos.[13]

13. Christian Smith with Melissa Lundquist Denton, *Soul Searching* (New York: Oxford University Press, 2005), pp. 223–224.

HOW I New Creation (15 minutes)

The Big Idea: Responding to God's grace transforms us and enables us to live out our sexual identities in ways that reflect our relationship with God.

> You'll need—
> • Copies of the *New Creation* handout (on DVD) or Student Journal (**page 33**)
> • Pencils

Explain: **Let's get even more personal in thinking about our sexual identities. What issues are you dealing with, and how could an understanding of God's Good/Guilt/Grace/Gratitude Story help you?**

At this point distribute copies of the *New Creation* handout (on DVD) or Student Journals and pencils to your students.

After they've finished jotting down (and perhaps sharing) their reflections, you might want to choose one of the options below to finish your discussion.

If most of your students identify themselves as Christians, we suggest that you invite your students to get into pairs or triplets and pray for each other.

> If any man is in Christ, he is a new creation (some assembly required).

If most of your students don't yet identify themselves as Christians, or if you're not sure, this might be a great chance to invite them to consider embracing God's story as their own.

If you have a pretty even mix between those who do and those who do not identify themselves as Christians, you might want to challenge them to face off in a rousing match of tug-of-war. Just kidding. Instead, it might be more appropriate to play some worship music and create an environment conducive to personal reflection, with plenty of time for students to think and be still before God. You may want to have some adults (parents and small group leaders) ready to pray individually with students who'd like to do so.

If you sense that guilt is a dominant issue with your students, you might want to skip ahead to the **Do-Overs** session on **pages 217–247**.

Other Resources for Teaching on Sexual Identity

NOW | SexTalk: Sexual Identity (15 minutes)

The Big Idea: Our hormones and our environment not only shape our sexual identities, but they also raise new questions and tensions.

Play the DVD, then ask—

Q: What in this video stood out to you? Why do you think that is?

Q: The video describes three boys in a locker room; one who wears no towel, one who clutches his towel, and one who has no need for a towel because he's never going near a shower. What do these three boys have in common? What makes them different?

Q: How would you define a person's sexual identity?

Q: What, if anything, is the difference between being a "sexual" person and being a "sexy" person?

Q: The video mentions a number of things that shape a person's sexual identity. What were some of those things?

Q: What else shapes a person's sexual identity?

Q: The video describes the Church as generally being either silent about sexuality or screaming itself hoarse. Talk about that.

At this point distribute pencils and copies of *SexTalk: Sexual Identity* (**on DVD**) to your students or have students turn to **page 36** of the Student Journal and invite them to reflect and respond to the provocative issues raised by the video.

> You'll need—
> • A television or video projection unit
> • DVD player
> • The *Good Sex* DVD, cued to "SexTalk: Sexual Identity"
> • Copies of the *SexTalk: Sexual Identity* handout (on DVD) or Student Journal (**page 36**)
> • Pencils
>
> If you have a talented actor or reader in your group, he or she could read "SexTalk: Sexual Identity" instead of you playing the DVD. The video transcript is on the DVD.

NOW | Boys Will Be and Girls Will Be (25 minutes)

The Big Idea: Much of our sexual identity has been shaped by members of our own gender, as well as folks from that sometimes wacky other gender.

You'll need—
• Poster paper or two whiteboards
• Pens

Welcome your students and ask the girls to sit on one side of the room and the guys to sit on the other side—or maybe even separate rooms. Give poster paper or a whiteboard, as well as pens, to both the girls and the guys.

Ask the guys to write down their answers to two questions: *What do guys think girls are like?* and *What do guys think guys are like?* Similarly, ask the girls to write down their answers to two questions: *What do girls think guys are like?* and *What do girls think girls are like?*

After each group has finished listing their answers, have them present their ideas to the other gender.

Q: What on these lists confirms what you would have expected?

FYI: According to a study of 1,017 seventh and eighth graders (conducted by the University of North Carolina School of Medicine, Chapel Hill), the more satisfied students are with their bodies, the higher their self-esteem.

Reuters, "Self-Esteem Tied to Body Image for Most Teens," msnbc.com (May 2007). (Article no longer available online.)

Q: What surprises you about these lists?

Q: How different do you think the two genders are?
• No different
• A bit different
• Fairly different
• Way different

Q: I'm going to read a series of questions. If your answer is "Yes," I want you to move to the left side of the room. If your answer is "No," I want you to move to the right side of the room. After each question, I'll see if any of you want to explain your answers.
• Is it really true that girls are more emotional?
• Are girls more serious about their relationships?
• Do you think guys are really less mature?

- Do guys evaluate girls primarily by their physical appearance, while girls focus more on guys' internal qualities?
- Are guys more interested in sex than girls are?

Q: What do you think is the one thing that boys most want to know about girls?

Q: What do you think is the one thing that girls most want to know about boys?

Explain: **Michael Gurian is a therapist with a lot of young clients. Here's his list of things that boys want to know:**
- How do I control myself?
- Why do I get so nervous around girls—does everyone, even athletic stars?
- How come he's got more hair than I do?
- Why do girls manipulate me so well?
- Will I ever get pubic hair?
- Am I big enough?
- How can I get more sex?
- Am I gay?
- Why do I feel ashamed of myself so much?[14]

Q: Do you think there's any question missing from this list?

Q: Most boys don't ask a therapist to answer these questions. Where do you think most boys get their answers?

Q: What questions do you think girls would love to ask about themselves?

Q: Where do you think most girls get their answers?

Transition to the next step by explaining: **I don't know about you, but I don't want my views of myself as a man or a woman to be determined solely by others around me. I want to know what makes me "me" on a deeper level.**

FYI: A 2007 report by the American Psychological Association spells out the destruction that comes from the pressures placed on girls to be "more sexy." Whether it's a five-year-old girl walking through a shopping mall in a short T-shirt that says "Juicy," or a magazine article that virtually promises teenage girls that losing 10 pounds will get them a boyfriend, or even a high school girls' volleyball coach who emphasizes players' sex appeal to draw bigger crowds, such sexualization is linked to impaired cognitive performance, eating disorders, low self-esteem, and even physical health problems.

Kara Powell and Brad Griffin, "New Twists on Not-So-New Issues for Girls," www.cyfm. net, http://www.cyfm.net/article.php?article=new_twists. html (accessed July 28, 2008).

14. Michael Gurian, *The Wonder of Boys* (New York: Tarcher/Putnam, 1997), p. 228.

NOW | Like Father, Like Son (15 minutes)

The Big Idea: Families in general, and maybe...*gasp...shudder...* even our own families, have molded our sexual identity.

Start by sharing one or two ways in which your parents have influenced you. Maybe you laugh "just like" your dad, or you respond to stress "exactly like" your mom.

You'll need—
• Copies of the *Like Father, Like Son* handout (on DVD) or Student Journal (**page 38**)
• Pencils

Q: Just like I've been shaped by my family, we all learn things from our families that establish, reinforce, or challenge our sexual identities. *(If you want to give an example, a few to choose from are "boys are tough" or "girls are emotional.")* What are some of the things we're taught about our sexual identities by the following relationships? *(Note: you don't have to go through all of them; you can select what you consider the most applicable.)*

- Father/Stepfather to son
- Father/Stepfather to daughter
- Mother/Stepmother to daughter
- Mother/Stepmother to son
- Brother to brother
- Brother to sister
- Sister to sister
- Sister to brother

Q: What are the *most* helpful messages about sexual identity you've received from your family?

For even more personal reflection or discussion, use the questions from *Like Father, Like Son* **(on DVD)**, or in the Student Journal on **page 38**, in a large group, small group, or individual setting.

NEW | The "H" Word (25 minutes)

The Big Idea: In the midst of the heated controversy about homosexuality, you can help your students work through some relevant Scripture passages.

Note to Youth Leader: We bring up the question of homosexuality because we know your students wonder about it. We don't claim to have all the answers, but we hope this discussion will be helpful to you—and more importantly, to your students. Please remember that just as the Christian community is divided over this issue, your students are probably also divided. Since not all denominations agree on this issue, nor do all churches within a denomination, nor do all people within a single church, it seems likely that your group of students will be somewhat fractured as well. Having said that, we encourage you to make sure that you understand your denomination's or church's views toward homosexuality before launching into this discussion with your students.

> **You'll need—**
> • Copies of *The "H" Word* handout (on DVD) or *The Grass Is Browner* handout (on DVD), or Student Journal (**pages 39-40**)
> • Pencils

Q: Which statement best describes your opinion?
☐ I think homosexuals are born, not made.
☐ I think homosexuals are made, not born.
☐ I don't think I know why some people are homosexual.

Choose three students who replied to each of these responses who'd be willing to complete these statements:
☐ I agreed that homosexuals are born, not made because...
☐ I agreed that homosexuals are made, not born because...
☐ I agreed that I don't know why some people are homosexual because...

Q: How many of you actually know people who describe themselves as homosexual? What about someone who's bisexual or transgender?

Q: For those of you who responded in the affirmative, how do these people feel about their sexuality?

> **FYI:** At the time of this writing, the research regarding the influence of biological forces in the development of sexual identity (especially homosexuality identity) is inconclusive.

Q: Are you well acquainted with someone who doesn't describe herself as a homosexual but you think she probably is?

FYI: One term your students will probably be familiar with—and therefore, you should be too—is LGBT: Lesbian, Gay, Bisexual, Transgender. *Gay* and *Lesbian* refer to same-gender sexual attraction; *Bisexual* refers to sexual attraction to both genders; *Transgender* refers to sexual identification with a gender other than the biological one. Today many schools (around 10 percent of public high school campuses, by some estimates) have LGBT clubs and gatherings.

FYI: According to the Centers for Disease Control, in the last decade, the number of women reporting a same-gender sexual experience has tripled, with much of that increase occurring in teenagers and women in their 20s. (Sexual Behavior and Selected Health Measures: Men and Women 15-44 Years of Age, United States, 2002)

• If so, what makes you think that person is a homosexual?

Q: Maybe you've heard the phrase "gay-dar," which tends to reflect someone's intuitive sense that another person is gay or bisexual. Do you think there's any validity to that idea? Why or why not?

• In your experience, is someone who's "metrosexual" (generally meaning a guy greatly concerned over his appearance) more or less likely to be homosexual?

Q: Increasingly, homosexual relationships seem to be more acceptable in our society. The cover of the October 10, 2005 issue of *Time* magazine had an article titled, "The Battle Over Gay Teens" with the subtitle of "They are coming out earlier, to a more accepting society." Do you think that subtitle is true? Talk about that.

Q: In a recent nationwide study of teenagers, 4.3 percent of 15-to-19-year-old boys and 10.7 percent of girls in the same age range said they'd had same-sex relations.[15] Based on what you hear from your friends and at your school, do you think the actual percentages are higher or lower?

Q: What do you think Scripture would say about this issue? Do you know any passages offhand that relate to homosexuality?

If your students need some hints on biblical passages, try pointing them to Genesis 19:1-17, Leviticus 18:1-30, Romans 1:18–2:15, and 1 Corinthians 6:9-11.

---

15. Mark Regnerus, *Forbidden Fruit* (New York: Oxford University Press, 2007), pp. 76–77.

Q: How do those Scripture verses affect your view of homosexuality?

Q: It's been said that even though there aren't many Scripture texts related to homosexuality, the few texts that do exist unambiguously condemn homosexuality. What do you think about that?

Q: In the same recent nationwide study mentioned above, teenagers whose religion was very important in their lives were less likely to have had same-sex relations. Why do you think that is?

• Is it only because of these Scripture passages, or are there other factors involved?

Q: It's been said that given the other sins described in many of these Scripture passages, homosexuality is no worse than any other sin, including heterosexual lust. What do you think of that argument?

Q: Do you think there's a difference between homosexual *curiosity* and homosexual *identity*? Talk about that.

• How about between homosexual *tendencies* and *acting* on those tendencies?

Read Ezekiel 16:46-52 with your students, then use the following questions for discussion.

Q: What do you think is the big idea here? Talk about that.

A thought about Ezekiel 16:46-52—

> God said the people of Israel (that's God's subject in this passage) were so bad that they made the wrongdoers in Samaria and Sodom look like Girl Scouts. Most of Ezekiel 16 is an extended metaphor in which God rescues and nurtures Israel as an infant child, raises her to adulthood, and then marries her as an act of committed love—only to watch her turn into a raging sex addict who sleeps with everyone but her own husband. Despite her great beauty, she actually pays men to sleep with her, driving her husband mad. It's a vivid picture.
>
> Here's the kicker: With this image of sexual debauchery and craziness, God says his beloved Israel is acting worse than Sodom ever did. Oddly enough, God doesn't say a word about sex when he talks about Sodom (which is, of course, world renowned for sex). God's beef with Sodom is that she was arrogant, overfed,

and unconcerned. She failed to help the poor. She was haughty and disgusting. But God doesn't mention "sodomy." This isn't to say that the violent lustiness of the men of Sodom in Genesis 18 and 19 wasn't a big deal. The results speak for themselves. But sex isn't what Ezekiel uses to make his point about how bad the Israelites were.

FYI: According to a 2007 study of participants in 16 different "ex-gay" programs, people who were highly motivated to move away from their gay tendencies experienced modest changes in their sexual attractions. Interestingly, the decreases they experienced in homosexual attraction were more significant than their increases in heterosexual attraction.

Tim Stafford, "An Older, Wiser Ex-Gay Movement," *Christianity Today*, October 2007, p. 49, http://www.christianitytoday.com/ct/2007/october/6.48.html (accessed July 28, 2008).

Q: What do you think about what I've just said? Talk about that.

• Where do you agree? Talk about that.

• Where do you disagree? Talk about that.

Q: Why do you think Sodom is more widely known for Genesis 18 and 19 than Ezekiel 16? Talk about that.

Q: As one preacher puts it, for every person who struggles with the sins of Sodom, there are nine who struggle with the sins of Samaria. What do you think that means?

Q: Some churches have the reputation for being unwelcoming to homosexuals, insisting that they change their lifestyle before they become a part of the church community. Other churches welcome homosexuals just as they are and don't require that they change their behavior or lifestyle at all. Still others welcome homosexuals into the church community but exclude them from leadership. What do you think of these three positions?

• What do you think God thinks of them?

• If you were in charge of a church, what would you hope its approach to homosexuals would be?

• What would be your stand on gay marriage?

• How about same-sex civil unions?

Q: Some Christians believe that ministry to homosexuals begins with loving them and getting to know them. Others believe it begins with telling them they're disobeying God. What do you think of these two starting points?

• If you had a friend who was homosexual (and many of you do), how would you begin your ministry?

Q: You've probably heard the phrase, "Love the sinner and hate the sin." When it comes to homosexuality, one youth ministry has decided to adopt "Love the sinner and hate your own sin" as their motto. What are the advantages and disadvantages of embracing that as your motto when it comes to homosexuality (or anything else, for that matter)?

To dive even further and more personally into the topic of homosexuality, use the questions found on the The "H" Word (on DVD) or The Grass Is Browner (on DVD) or Student Journal **pages 39-40**, as material for large or small group discussion, or individual personal reflection.

> It took me a long time to learn that God is not the enemy of my enemies. He's not even the enemy of His own enemies!
> — Martin Niemöller, a German pastor imprisoned by the Nazis for eight years
>
> Roy B. Zuck, The Speaker's Quote Book (Grand Rapids, Mich.: Kregel Publications, 1997), p. 130.

NEW I Fruit: A Manly Meal or a Feminine Treat? (25 minutes)

The Big Idea: The fruit of the Spirit shows up in our lives after we have a personal relationship with God, regardless of our gender.

You'll need—
• One piece of fruit for each student
• Copies of the *Fruit: A Manly Meal or a Feminine Treat?* handout (on DVD) or Student Journal (**page 41**)
• Pencils

Give an opportunity for those who want a piece of fruit to choose one. Read Galatians 5:22-23 with your students. Highlight how Paul refers to the fruit of the Spirit, meaning its work that the Spirit does in us. It's not fruit that comes from merely our own efforts or will. Our efforts and will are involved, but the fruit is ultimately a result of the Spirit flowing through us.

Q: In this passage Paul lists the well-known "fruit of the Spirit." Do you think of the attributes in Galatians 5:22-23 as more masculine or more feminine?

	More feminine because...	More masculine because...	Both feminine and masculine because...
Love			
Joy			
Peace			
Patience			
Kindness			
Goodness			
Faithfulness			
Gentleness			
Self-control			

Q: Do you think most people in our culture seem confused or rather clear about what's masculine and what's feminine?

Q: Do you think Jesus was more masculine or more feminine?

Read Galatians 3:26-29 with your students.

Explain: **Jesus combined what we call masculine and feminine traits in a comfortable balance of humanness. He hugged children and spoke up for them in Mark 10:13-16. He got physical with merchants who exploited poor people in the temple in John 2:13-22. He was tough on people who were full of themselves in John 5:41-47. He cried over the grief of a friend in John 11:35. Jesus was not a stereotypical, testosterone-crazed man, and he wasn't a sissy. In a culture where children were disposable and women would have been second-class citizens—had they been allowed to be citizens at all— Jesus respected children and treated women as equals. And the spirit of Jesus, the Holy Spirit, produces fruit in every believer's life as if gender had nothing to do with anything.**

The fruit of the Spirit is love, joy, peace, patience, kindness, goodness, faithfulness, gentleness, and self-control. When it comes to our sexual identity, God's Spirit nullifies "boys will be boys" and "women—can't live with 'em, can't live without 'em." The Holy Spirit replaces roughness with gentleness and transforms compulsiveness into self-control. Not quickly, perhaps, but inevitably.

This isn't to say there's no difference between men and women, only that the differences have nothing to do with character, giftedness, or fruitfulness. Does this make sense in our culture where people are stereotyped from the moment of birth? Not really. But so what? As Jesus put it to Nicodemus in John 3:8, "The wind blows wherever it pleases. You hear its sound, but you cannot tell where it comes from or where it is going. So it is with everyone born of the Spirit." The people of God—male and female—are freaks; we don't fit cultural norms because we're coming from another place. Our passports are issued in the kingdom of heaven where we're—every one of us by God's grace—naturalized citizens.

That means that in our culture, women may be considered masculine and men may be thought feminine for exhibiting characteristics that are merely godly. And it breaks our hearts (on those days when it doesn't make us

angry) that these characterizations are about as common inside the family of God as outside. We can't control what outsiders say about us, but shame on us for choosing cultural stereotypes over biblical models of transformation and growth. That's just plain wrong.

Q: In what ways does our society force gender norms onto us?

Q: In Galatians 3:26-29 is Paul saying that when we become followers of Jesus Christ we lose those things that make us male and female?

Q: What do you think he's getting at?

Q: What do you think we have to gain or lose by treating each other first as humans made in God's image, and then as male and female? Talk about that.

Q: What do you think we have to gain or lose if we accept or pass on the gender norms of our culture? Talk about that.

FYI: Feel free to point out that it's difficult to find any statement about the equality of the sexes, however weak, in any ancient texts. That is, except for those of Christianity. In the midst of a culture in which women fared poorly, Paul levels the two genders based on who we are before Christ.

To help students further examine their own perspective on femininity, masculinity, fruit of the Spirit, and the relationship between them all, use the questions found on the *Fruit: A Manly Meal or a Feminine Treat?* handout (on DVD), or Student Journal **page 41**, in a large group, small group, or as a tool for individual personal reflection.

HOW | That's Gotta Hurt (20 minutes)

The Big Idea: Tragic circumstances affect our sexual identities.

Explain: **You've probably heard the expression "sticks and stones may break my bones, but names will never hurt me." Unfortunately, that's far from the truth. Our experiences—even those of the non-bone-breaking variety—can hurt us.** At this point, you might share a personal experience in which you were hurt and how that affects you still today.

> You'll need—
> • Copies of the *That's Gotta Hurt* handout (on DVD) or Student Journal (**page 45**)
> • Pencils
> • A hammer
> • A piece of wood
> • A nail

Q: Without naming names, do you know anyone who's suffered from negative verbal abuse? Can you tell this person's story?

Q: With this in mind, what effect do you think verbal and emotional abuse might have on a person's sexual identity?

At this point hold up the piece of wood and explain that it can represent any one of us. The nail represents the painful circumstances in our lives. Ask for a volunteer (probably a more mature student; you don't want a smirking ninth-grade boy to cheapen the illustration) to use the hammer to tap the nail a few times into the piece of wood. Then remove the nail so a small hole remains in the wood.

Q: What effect do you think a physical disability might have on a person's sexual identity? Talk about that.

Q: What effect do you think sexual molestation might have on a person's sexual identity?

At this point have the same or a different volunteer hammer the nail into the wood again but in a different section to create a new hole.

Q: What effect do you think rape might have on a person's sexual identity?

Q: What effect do you think incest might have on a person's sexual identity?

At this point have the volunteer make another small hole in the wood.

Q: Can you think of any other circumstances that might have a real effect on our sexual identities?

Q: Do you have any close friends or family members who've suffered in any of these ways? How do you think they cope, if at all, with the effects?

Hold up the piece of wood to your students and ask—**What do you think Jesus might want to say to the people you've been thinking about?**

Q: What effect does Jesus have on the ways our circumstances have affected our sexual identities?

Read Psalm 42:5 and ask—**What does it look like to be downcast about circumstances that have hurt us but then put our hope in the Lord? Is it possible to be downcast *while* having our hope in the Lord? Or does hoping in the Lord eliminate our grief and sadness?**

To help students further understand the way their sexual identities have been affected by painful experiences, use the questions included in *That's Gotta Hurt* **(on DVD)**, or Student Journal **page 45**, for large or small group discussions, as well as for individual personal reflection.

If it's appropriate in your context, conclude with some time for prayer and worship in the midst of, or after, the students' reflection time. You might even want to invite students who feel a special need for healing to approach another student or an adult for a focused time of prayer. Make sure that in the midst of acknowledging past and present pain, you also point students to Jesus as their ultimate source of hope and healing.

HOW | Divorce and Us (15 minutes)

The Big Idea: Divorce affects our sexual identity and gives us unique opportunities to experience God.

Explain: **There's one experience shared by many of us here that definitely affects our own views of ourselves and our views of God: divorce. The projected divorce rate for first marriages is now about 43 percent. When divorced folks get remarried, about 60 percent of those marriages end up as divorces.**

Tragically, the first marriages of children from divorced parents are more likely to end in divorce (approximately 60 percent will end in divorce versus 43 percent for the general population). So because of how divorce is affecting you now, and how divorce might affect you in the future, it's never too soon or too late to talk about it together.

You'll need—
• In advance arrange to have two volunteers (either adults or mature students) share their experiences related to divorce. One volunteer should be the child of divorce; the other volunteer should have a good friend who is the child of divorce.
• Also invite some parents—both those who've been divorced and those who haven't— to come and pray with your students.

Invite the volunteer who is the child of divorce to come and share his or her story in order to put a human face to the statistics you've just given. Afterward ask your group:

Q: What in our friend's story confirms what you might have expected?

Q: What in this story surprises you?

Q: For those of you who also have parents who've been divorced, what elements of your story are important to add to what we've just heard?

Explain that even if students don't have parents who've been divorced, they have friends who have divorced parents. Invite the volunteer who has a good friend with divorced parents to share about how divorce has affected that friend.

Q: What elements of this story have you seen in your own friends with divorced parents?

> "The notion of systemic abandonment is not limited to those external systems originally designed to nurture, protect, and help shape a unique adolescent. Another perhaps more subtle yet far more insidious form of abandonment has occurred that has had a devastating effect on the adolescent psyche and landscape. Adolescents have suffered the loss of safe relationships and intimate settings that served as the primary nurturing community for those traveling the path from child to adult. The most obvious example of this is in the family. The postmodern family is often so concerned about the needs, struggles, and issues of parents that the emotional and developmental needs of the children go largely unmet."

Chap Clark, *Hurt* (Grand Rapids, Mich.: Baker Academic, 2004), p. 50.

Q: What experiences have your friends who're children of divorce had that weren't part of this story but are still important for us to think about?

At this point you could note that according to Elizabeth Marquardt's study of 1,500 young adults between ages 18 and 35, children of divorce often report feeling like they're the glue trying to keep a family unit together. They also often feel like they have divided selves, since they have a whole different life with each parent, and it's one they cannot share with the other parent.[16]

Q: How do you think having divorced parents affects the sexual identity of a person (including maybe you or some of your friends)?

Q: Some of your friends might not have divorced parents, but they have parents who are emotionally absent and disengaged. Some of your friends—and some of you, for that matter—likely feel abandoned as a result. How do you think that disengagement affects people's sexual identities?

Conclude by creating an environment that is conducive to reflection and prayer. Explain: **I've invited some parents to join us. Some have been divorced, and some have not. Regardless of their backgrounds, they care about you, and they'd be happy to pray for you or for a friend of yours that you've been thinking about during this session.**

16. Elizabeth Marquardt, *Between Two Worlds* (New York: Three Rivers Press, 2006).

SESSION 3

For Your Own Preparation

Sex does not equal intimacy. Intimacy equals intimacy.

Intimacy grows between people who trust each other with their deepest natures. Intimacy rejects fakery and shortcuts. There's no such thing as instant intimacy—instant attraction, yes; instant crushes, of course; but real intimacy takes time.

Intimacy isn't a feeling; it's a condition. Intimacy takes time and attention and energy. To some people, that sounds a lot like work. So, sometimes people do things to *feel* intimate, even if they aren't.

It doesn't take a genius to understand what happens when people pretend to be intimate: Intimacy Lite—less filling, but still intoxicating in sufficient quantities.

It also doesn't take a genius to understand why people might settle for Intimacy Lite. True intimacy is risky. Being intimate means facing the possibility of rejection and embarrassment. That's why intimacy is so hard: because it's a high-risk investment. So, after we get hurt a couple of times, most of us learn to lay back and play it safe, investing a little of our true selves, but not enough to risk a serious loss.

It's a good strategy, except for the fact that humans need intimacy—whether we want it or not.

> Fool me once, shame on you; fool me twice, shame on me.

Right from the start (Genesis 2:18), God declared that humans shouldn't be alone; we need help to make it.

God said, plain as day, that it's not good for humans to be isolated. Most of us know instinctively that God is right about this. Dangerous as it is, what people crave—perhaps more than anything else—is authentic intimacy.

This is your heart.
This is your heart broken.
Any questions?

But it turns out that sex can be a handy substitute for authentic intimacy.

There's no question that sex feels intimate. You're breathing the same air, sharing the same space, being glued together sexually—"glued together" is how the Bible puts it when it says two people are united as "one flesh." (See Genesis 2:24; Matthew 19:5-6; Mark 10:7-8; 1 Corinthians 6:16; and Ephesians 5:31. Translated as *cleave* in the King James Version and *united* in the TNIV, the word means, "to glue together.") It's hard to get any closer than that.

FYI: Teenage girls' first sexual partner is generally one to three years older than them. The younger the girl is when she first has sexual intercourse, the more sexual partners she's likely to have.

J. C. Abma, G. M. Martinez, W. D. Mosher, and B. S. Dawson, "Teenagers in the United States: Sexual Activity, Contraceptive Use, and Childbearing, 2002 Statistics," *Vital Health Stat* 23, no. 24 (2004): 1–48.

But when a relationship comes unglued, so do the feelings. And sometimes the people come apart as well.

Do you ever wonder why dating—the way most of us do it—doesn't work very well? Why the shortest distance between a blissful crush and wishing you'd never met someone is going out with that person? (This is just a general observation; skip this part if you think you're the exception to the rule.)

John: "You slept with her?"
Richard: "Don't worry; it wasn't intimate."
—*Ally McBeal*, "Hope and Glory" episode, Fox Television

Many in our culture believe intimacy leads inevitably to sex. "You can't get that close to people without going farther," they say. And by going farther, they mean getting sexual. This is intimacy as foreplay, and it's highly toxic to otherwise healthy friendships. (Have you noticed how when people get sexually involved with their close friends, they tend to drift apart afterward?) There goes the possibility of friendship between men and women. Too bad.

The Bible describes us (Christians, at least) as brothers and sisters. Sorry, but there are things healthy brothers and sisters don't do, and it's not because they're not intimate.

Even same-gender intimacy is threatened by the assumption or fear that people can't get close without getting busy with each other. Not everybody makes that assumption—not by a long shot. It's crazy and unfair. But it's there like a rumor, isolating people, making them uncomfortable and suspicious and separate. Again: too bad.

It's not supposed to be like this because it's not good for people to be isolated. God said so.

Reflect for a Moment

We can't lead students where we're not willing to go ourselves. We can point them... but they'd rather be guided. Here are a few questions to consider as you prepare to lead this session on intimacy.

Q: When you were 15, what did you think *intimacy* meant?

• Where did you get those ideas?

Q: How have your thoughts about intimacy changed?

Q: What are some words that characterize your most intimate relationships, past and present?

Q: Have you experienced intimacy that seems unhealthy to you now?

Q: What has romance added or subtracted in your experience of intimacy?

Q: What are your future hopes for intimacy?

Q: If you had just one hour to talk with kids about intimacy, what would you try to communicate?

• Why do you think that's so important?

• If you couldn't lecture on the subject, how would you try to communicate during that hour?

NOW | SexTalk: Intimacy (15 minutes)

The Big Idea: Sex does not equal intimacy. Intimacy equals intimacy. It's time we learned that for good.

Play the DVD, then ask—

Q: What idea or phrase stuck with you from that piece?

Q: Why do you think that's significant?

Q: Without naming names, do you recognize Sophie's dilemma from observation or personal experience? Someone who's seen the cycle—tell us how it ends.

Q: Talk about why you agree or disagree with the statement that people sometimes attempt to substitute sex for intimacy.

Q: What's the problem with sexualizing intimacy between friends?

• Has anyone ever said that you or someone you know is a homosexual because you have a deeply intimate friendship? Someone who's had that experience—tell us how that affected you.

Transition: **We'll talk about the brother + sister imagery in the Bible in a little bit. Right now, let's spend a few minutes looking at an interesting connection in 1 Thessalonians.**

You'll need—
• A television or video projection unit
• DVD player
• The *Good Sex* DVD, cued to "SexTalk: Intimacy"

If you have a talented actor or reader in your group, he or she could read "SexTalk: Intimacy" instead of playing the DVD. The video transcript is on the DVD.

NEW | Friends with Benefits (20 minutes)

The Big Idea: We have a mandate to love each other as we want to be loved.

Distribute the handout.

You'll need—
- Bibles
- Copies of the *Friends with Benefits* handout (on DVD) or Student Journal (**page 52**)
- Pencils

Explain: **In just a moment, I'm going to read eight statements, and when I say "Go," I want you to move to a place in the room that most nearly reflects where you stand on each statement:**
- **The far (or left) end of the room means you disagree completely.**
- **The middle means you're not sure where you stand or you'd rather not say.**
- **The near (or right) end of the room means you agree completely.**

I'll read each statement and when I say "Go," you'll have five seconds to move and find a partner at your new location.

Read the first statement.

Statement 1: I've seen someone wronged or taken advantage of in a relationship.

Ready? Go.

When students arrive at their positions, say: **Get a partner and take 30 seconds each to tell why you agree, disagree, or can't say.**

Time them as precisely as you wish.

Okay, next statement:

Statement 2: I've been personally wronged or taken advantage of in a relationship.

You have five seconds to move and find a partner. Ready? Go.

Take 30 seconds each to tell why you agree, disagree, or can't say.

Okay, next statement—you know what to do:

Read the remaining statements from the handout and direct students through the process. When you complete the statements on the handout…

Invite everyone to sit down and think through some questions together.

Q: Were there any uncomfortable moments for you in this process? Why is that?

• Were there any surprises? Talk about that.

Read 1 Thessalonians 4:1-8 together.

Q: What stands out to you in these verses? Talk about why you think those ideas are significant

Explain: **Are you familiar with the term *sanctified*? When something is *sanctified* that means it's been set apart from ordinary use and reserved for God's exclusive possession.**

Q: How would you characterize the examples Paul uses to explain what he means when he tells the Thessalonian Christians it's God's will that they should be sanctified?

Q: If people are true friends—spiritual brothers and sisters, for example—what happens to the intimacy if they take advantage of each other sexually?

Explain: **In English, we pretty much have one word for love. Does anyone know what that word is? Right, it's *love*. I love my friends, I love my family, I love my phone, I love pizza… The language in which the New Testament was written is somewhat richer in this regard. Ancient Greek has four different words to describe four distinct kinds of love.**

> FYI: A thorough reading of 1 Thessalonians 4:1-2 teaches an important truth about sanctification. Paul affirms the Thessalonians for the way they're already making choices that please God, and yet he asks and urges that they "do this more and more." Zeroing in on their sexual behavior may be a clue that they were—as William Barclay puts it—having trouble unlearning what they had for all of their lives accepted as natural in a society where chastity was an unknown virtue. Whether it be greed, violence, sexual conduct, or any other area of our lives, sanctification is a process that involves continual growth and ongoing choices.

> FYI: "Friends with benefits" is one way of describing friends (at various levels of true intimacy) who sexualize their relationships from time to time without identifying themselves as a couple.

Look at the four kinds of love and the C. S. Lewis quote on the handout.

Q: What does the term *friends with benefits* mean in your culture?

Q: Which of the four loves is expressed in a "friends with benefits" relationship?

• How about in a casual hook up? Which kind of love is that? Anybody here ever seen a hook up turn out badly?

Q: If you've known anyone in a friends-with-benefits relationship—without identifying them—tell us how you think that turned out long-term (or how you think it's *going* to turn out).

Return to the questions on the handout.

When you complete the handout…

Q: How do you think the passage we read in 1 Thessalonians speaks to friends with benefits?

Explain: **Bible scholars say the new Christians Paul wrote to in Thessalonica grew up in a culture where the idea of sexual self-control was a novelty. In general, it was a society where people did pretty much as they pleased. So, being *sanctified* to God was a new idea that would have taken some getting used to. Does that sound at all familiar?**

What if we turned the idea of friends with benefits upside down? What if we said the greatest benefit friends can share isn't *comfort sex* or *recreational sex* but genuine Agape-style intimacy? Intimacy that's about giving and not getting?

Q: Do you think the people you know would find that idea appealing? Talk about that.

• Do you think this group would grow or shrink if we became known as the place to find true intimacy that doesn't get all tangled up with sex? And you think that because…

Transition: **Let's spend the rest of this session thinking about how we can look out for one another.**

HOW I One Another (20 minutes)

The Big Idea: Intimate relationships in the context of the "one another" passages in Scripture

Distribute the *One Another* handout.

You'll need—
• List-making supplies
• Copies of the *One Another* handout (on DVD) or Student Journal **(page 56)**
• Pencils

Explain: **I'm going to read some of the passages in the Bible that use the term *one another* (or something really close to it). There are lots more than just** these, but we'd be here all day if we read them all. Circle or underline the "one another" commands on your handout, and I'll write them on our list.

Read (or have someone read) the "one another" verses and work through the questions together.

As people identify the "one another" commands, write the actions on your list (for example, "don't lie," "show mercy").

When you reach the end of the handout...

Q: What could get in the way of building this kind of "one another" community with each other?

• How would our group look different if it were bursting with examples of these "one another" commands?

• How would our friendships look different if we put these things into practice?

• How would our dating relationships look different if we took these commands seriously and seriously trusted God to energize us to live them out?

Q: What do you think it would take for us to get this "one another" in gear? Let's make a list:
   • What do you think we might need to start doing?
   • What do you think we might need to stop doing?
   • Where do you think we might get what it takes to do that for each other?

Conclude: Invite the group to spend a few minutes talking with God in silence.

At any time, invite them to get up and put their initials on the lists you've made together.

Close with a prayer of hope that God will create genuinely healing, energizing, intimate relationships in your group.

The best definition of faith I ever heard was Paul Tillich when he said, "Faith is the courage to accept acceptance." Meaning? Faith is a code to accept that Jesus knows my whole life story, every skeleton in my closet, every moment of sin, shame, dishonesty, degradedness darkening my past. Right now he knows my shallow faith, my feeble prayer life, my inconsistent discipleship, and he comes beside me and he says, I dare you to trust. I dare you to trust that I love you, just as you are and not as you should be, because you're never going to be as you should be.
— Brennan Manning, *Christianity Today* interview

"The Dick Staub Interview: Brennan Manning on Ruthless Trust," *Christianity Today*, December 1, 2002, http://www.christianitytoday.com/ct/2002/decemberweb-only/12-9-21.0.html?start=2 (accessed July 29, 2008).

Other Resources for Teaching on Intimacy

NOW | Intimacy (15 minutes)

The Big Idea: Exploring attitudes about intimacy—real and imagined

Play the video, then ask—

Q: Which comments on this video reflect the views and attitudes of your friends and other kids at school?

Q: What comment resonated with what you think about intimacy?

Q: Where would you guess that some of these people got their ideas about intimacy?

Distribute the *Intimacy* handout and work through the questions together.

When you finish the handout…

Conclude this element by inviting everyone to join hands and ask God to teach you the lessons you need to learn about intimacy.

You'll need—
• A television or video projection unit
• DVD player
• The *Good Sex* DVD, cued to "Intimacy"
• Copies of the *Intimacy* handout (on DVD) or Student Journal (**page 59**)
• Pencils

Instead of playing the DVD, with a little preparation, you can have students perform "Intimacy." The video transcript is on the DVD.

FYI: In a 2005 report, fewer than half of all ninth through twelfth grade students reported having had sexual intercourse, reflecting a decline during the last decade from 53 percent in 1993 to 47 percent in 2003. Males were more likely than females to report having had sexual intercourse.

Kaiser Family Foundation, "U.S. Teen Sexual Activity," January 2005, http://www.kff.org/youthhivstds/upload/U-S-Teen-Sexual-Activity-Fact-Sheet.pdf (accessed July 29, 2008).

NOW I Love Stories (30 minutes)

The Big Idea: First-person stories about growing intimacy

Invite an adult couple whose relationship you really admire to answer these questions during the session. Prepare them before they're in front of the group, asking that they be as real and honest as possible. Ask them to please not preach, but tell their stories directly and trust you to help the students process the meaning. (Agree on a signal to use if you think they're going on too long about a question.)

You'll need—
• An adult couple (or two), willing and able to answer honest questions about intimacy
• Copies of the *Love Stories* handout (on DVD) or Student Journal (**page 61**)
• Pencils

Q: In under a minute each, can you tell us how your love story began?

Q: What did you share in common at the beginning of your relationship?

Q: How did you first know this was someone you'd like to see more of?

Q: How long before you knew this was the one? How did you find that out?

Q: What were the biggest struggles you had while you were dating? How did you overcome them?

Q: What did your relationship bring you that you didn't have before?

Q: Where were you when you agreed to marry? On a scale of 1 (completely unromantic) to 10 (the most romantic thing ever), how romantic was that?

Q: What has your relationship taught you about intimacy? How did you learn those lessons?

Q: Do you think traditional dating is the best way to find your soul mate? Because…

Q: If you had just one paragraph to summarize all of this, what advice could you give us today about intimacy?

Thank your guests and excuse them so you can talk about them behind their backs. When they're no longer in the room, follow up with these discussion questions.

Q: What do you respect about that couple's relationship? Why?

Q: Do you think anything they shared about their early relationship is relevant today? What's no longer relevant?

Distribute the *Love Stories* handout and continue working through the questions together (or privately, if that seems better in the moment).

When you finish the handout, make a list...

Q: Let's list as many elements as we can recall that contribute to their happiness together (things like good communication, honesty, patience, time together...).

• Let's add some other ingredients that you think contribute to loving intimacy.

Q: How hard do you think it is to find really good examples of loving, intimate relationships that have lasted a long time?

Q: What are some things we can do right now to prepare for relationships that will remain intimate and long-lasting?

Conclude by inviting students to quietly approach the list you've made together and put their initials next to the items they want God to help them develop.

When you're ready, pray to close the session or transition to your next element.

NOW | Mistakes Girls Make (10 minutes)

The Big Idea: Girls make a lot of mistakes when they relate to guys.

Distribute the *Mistakes Girls Make* handout.

You'll need—
- List-making supplies
- Copies of the *Mistakes Girls Make* handout (on DVD) or Student Journal **(page 62)**
- Pencils

Explain: **Spend a couple minutes with the *Mistakes Girls Make* handout.**[17] **When I call you back, we'll make a list of mistakes we've seen girls make when they relate to guys—especially when they feel lonely or insecure.**

When you reconvene the group, write:

WHEN A GIRL IS LONELY OR INSECURE...

Then call out mistakes girls make from the handout and write them down in a word or a short phase as students vote...

Explain: **When I call out a mistake to add to the list, vote on whether you see that mistake:**
- **A—All the time**
- **S—Sometimes**
- **N—Almost never**

When you get to the end of the items on the handout, ask:

Q: Have you seen any other mistakes that we should add to the list? Raise your hand. I'll write them down, and you can vote Always, Sometimes, Almost never.

Next, write:

WHEN A GIRL LIKES A GUY...

And repeat the process of naming and voting and adding other things they've seen.

---

17. Adapted from Dr. Laura Schlessinger, *Ten Stupid Things Women Do to Mess Up Their Lives*, 1st Harper-Perennial ed., (New York: HarperCollins, 1995).

Now make the same kind of list with the heading:

WHEN A GIRL STARTS DATING A GUY...

Finally, make a list titled:

WHEN A GIRL GOES THROUGH A BREAKUP...

After you complete the final list, ask the group to explain:

Q: Why do you think girls make these mistakes?

Q: Which of these mistakes are the most costly in terms of sadness, self-doubt, and loss of self-esteem?

Q: What can a group like ours do to help girls recover from these mistakes?

• What can we do to help girls *avoid* these mistakes?

Conclude this element by inviting the girls to join hands in a circle. Ask the boys to place a hand respectfully on the shoulder of a young woman (promise to glare at them if they spoil this moment). Then pray for the girls, asking God to give them a sense of perspective about relationships that will protect them from doing harm or being harmed unnecessarily.

NOW | Mistakes Guys Make (10 minutes)

The Big Idea: Guys make a lot of mistakes when they relate to girls.

Distribute the *Mistakes Guys Make* handout.

You'll need—
• List-making supplies
• Copies of the *Mistakes Guys Make* handout (on DVD) or Student Journal (**page 64**)
• Pencils

Explain: **Spend a couple minutes with the *Mistakes Guys Make* handout.**[18] **When I call you back, we'll make a list of mistakes some guys make when they relate to girls—especially when they feel lonely or insecure.**

When you reconvene the group, write:
WHEN A GUY IS LONELY OR INSECURE...

Then call out mistakes guys make from the handout and write them down in a word or a short phase as students vote...

Explain: **When I call out a mistake to add to the list, vote on whether you see that mistake:**
• **A—All the time**
• **S—Sometimes**
• **N—Almost never**

When you get to the end of the items on the handout, ask:

Q: Have you seen any other mistakes we should add to the list? Raise your hand. I'll write them down, and you can vote Always, Sometimes, Almost never.

Next, write:
WHEN A GUY LIKES A GIRL...

And repeat the process of naming and voting and adding other things they've seen.

---

18. Adapted from Dr. Laura Schlessinger, *Ten Stupid Things Men Do to Mess Up Their Lives*, 1st HarperPerennial ed., (New York: HarperCollins, 1998).

Now make the same kind of list with the heading:

WHEN A GUY STARTS DATING A GIRL...

Finally, make a list titled:

WHEN A GUY GOES THROUGH A BREAKUP...

After you complete the final list, ask the group to explain:

Q: Why do you think guys make these mistakes?

Q: Which of these are the most costly in terms of sadness, self-doubt, and loss of self-esteem?

Q: What can a group like ours do to help guys recover from these mistakes?

• What can we do to help guys avoid these mistakes?

Conclude this element by inviting the guys to join hands in a circle (promise to glare at them if they spoil this moment). Ask the girls to place a hand respectfully on the shoulder of a young man. Then pray for the guys, asking God to give them a sense of perspective about relationships that will protect them from doing harm or being harmed unnecessarily.

NEW I One Is the Loneliest Number (30 minutes)

The Big Idea: Recognizing some relational red flags

Explain: **One of the most unusual people in the Bible was a man named Samson. Samson lived under something called the "Nazirite vow," which meant:**

1. He could not have wine or any product of a grapevine.
2. He could not cut his hair or beard.
3. He could not touch a dead body.
4. He could not eat food that was designated as unclean by Jewish dietary laws. (Judges 13:7; 16:17)

As long as he kept these four obligations, Samson was granted astounding physical strength.

But there was a problem. Samson—who was about as Jewish as a person can get—was fascinated by pagan women, including a Philistine woman he almost married in Judges 14, and Delilah whom we're about to meet in Judges 16.

Read Judges 16:4-22 with your two helpers. After the cheering dies down, ask:

Q: What words would you use to describe Delilah?

Q: How would you describe Delilah's effect on Samson and his vow to God?

• Go back and look at verses 1-3. Given what's there, how much blame do you think Delilah deserves compared to, I don't know…Samson?

Joke: I don't really have a follow-up question; I just want to take a moment to contemplate the weird fact that God sometimes works through idiots like Samson (and me!).

You'll need—
• Bibles
• Copies of the *One Is the Loneliest Number* handout (on DVD) or Student Journal (**page 66**)
• Pencils
• In advance ask a male and a female student to help you read Judges 16:4-22. The male student can read Samson's lines; the female can read Delilah's lines; you can narrate (take time for a couple of rehearsals).

Q: All right, moving on… Imagine you were there and that after the first or second time when Delilah tried to find out the secret to Samson's strength, he told you and some other friends what was happening with her. What advice would you give him?

• Do you believe that if Samson had you for a friend, this story might have turned out differently? Why?

• If one of your friends expressed concern about the quality of your current relationship, how do you think you'd react? Why?

Divide the room in half. Ask for a student volunteer on one side of the room to share an idea about how a dating relationship can help a person's relationship with God. Then ask for someone on the other side of the room to share an idea about how dating can harm a person's relationship with God—as it did with Samson. Go back and forth several times until you're eventually inviting students from both sides to contribute to both topics.

Distribute the *One Is the Loneliest Number* handout and pencils.

Explain: **I'm going to give you about five minutes to work on this handout. Then we'll continue together.**

When you reconvene the group conversation, talk through the handout together:

Conclude this element by inviting the group to take two minutes to write a short prayer on their handout (or in their Student Journal) about not allowing themselves to become isolated from friends who can help them think clearly about their sexual behavior.

When you're ready, close the session with a prayer of your own or transition to your next learning element.

FYI: In the National Longitudinal Study of Adolescent Health, 56.2 percent of African-American teenagers reported they were not virgins, in comparison with 33.9 percent of Latino teenagers, 33.4 percent of Caucasian teenagers, and 19.9 percent of Asian-American teenagers.

Mark Regnerus, *Forbidden Fruit* (New York: Oxford University Press, 2007), p. 122.

NEW | Best Buds (10 minutes)

The Big Idea: Intimacy begins with loyalty and a commitment to the best for another person.

Distribute the *Best Buds* handout and work through the questions together.

You'll need—
• Bibles
• Copies of the *Best Buds* handout (on DVD) or Student Journal (**page 68**)
• Pencils
• In advance recruit three students or leaders (two male, one female) to read 1 Samuel 20. The female will read the narrator lines, and the males will split the David and Jonathan lines.

When you finish the handout...

Explain: **In the passage we're about to read, Jonathan is the son of the king of Israel and first in line to succeed his father. Jonathan is also the best friend of David who's been unofficially named as the next king, even though he has no legal right to the title.**

Ask your three readers to read 1 Samuel 20 out loud.

Q: Whom do you identify with most in this story? Why is that?

• Whom would you least like to trade places with? Because...

Q: Have you had a friend like Jonathan?

• Have you *been* a friend like Jonathan?

FYI: Some theologians think Saul hurled his spear at Jonathan (v. 33) just because he was angry. Others think it's because David and Jonathan's friendship was so tight that they were one in Saul's mind.

Compare 1 Samuel 20 with 1 Corinthians 13:4-7.

Q: How do you think Jonathan and David stack up in the comparison?

• Compare your closest friendships with 1 Corinthians 13:4-7. How do you think you stack up?

• Do you see anything you could use some help with? Is there someone you know who may be able to help you?

Conclude this element by inviting everyone to gather close and stack hands (like in a sports team huddle) and follow you in echoing the following prayer:

God, I want to *be* the kind of friend I want to *have*.
Right here and right now,
I invite you, great God,
To do whatever it takes,
To grow me into the kind of person,
I would trust with my life.
And all God's people said, *Amen*.

NEW | The Yoke's on You (15 minutes)

The Big Idea: What does it mean to be unequally yoked to an unbeliever?

Read 2 Corinthians 6:14–7:1 together.

Explain: **The imagery of being yoked together unequally recalls the commandment in Deuteronomy 22:10 to not plow with an ox and donkey yoked together—there are some animals who just don't fit together because their body shapes are completely different.**

You'll need—
• Bibles
• Copies of *The Yoke's on You* handout (on DVD) or Student Journal (**page 70**)
• Pencils

FYI: Some people cite 2 Corinthians 6:14–7:1 as a reason Christians shouldn't go out with people who aren't Christians. In fact, some folks say Christians shouldn't partner in business—or even cultivate deep friendships—with people who don't pledge their allegiance to Christ.

Q: Do you think there's a difference between close friendship and being yoked together with another person? Talk about that.

Q: Do you think this passage means we shouldn't be friends with people who aren't Christians? How would you use what you know about other passages of Scripture to help explain your answer?

• Do you think an unequal yoke could make it difficult for you to lead another person to faith in Christ? Because...

Q: What reasons have you heard to explain why someone who loves Jesus shouldn't go out with someone who doesn't?

• What reasons have you heard to explain why it's okay for Christians to go out with people who are skeptical about the Christian faith?

Distribute *The Yoke's on You* handout and pencils.

Explain: **Take a few minutes to work on the handout, then we'll talk some more.**

When you're ready, talk through the questions on the handout.

Conclude by asking:

Q: If you can think of an area where you'd like to grow to become a better friend, write a brief series of steps that you think would help you get from where you are now to where you'd like to be (including getting support to help you grow).

FYI: The older the student, the more likely they are to have had sex. In 2003, 33 percent of ninth graders had had sexual intercourse, in comparison with 62 percent of twelfth graders.

Kaiser Family Foundation, "U.S. Teen Sexual Activity," January 2005, http://www.kff.org/youthhivstds/upload/U-S-Teen-Sexual-Activity-Fact-Sheet.pdf (accessed July 29, 2008).

NEW | To Wed or Not to Wed (15 minutes)

The Big Idea: It's not written anywhere that you *have* to get married.

Explain: **There's an interesting paragraph in 1 Corinthians 7 where Paul leaves the door to remaining single wide open.**

Read 1 Corinthians 7:8-9 together.

> You'll need—
> • Bibles
> • List-making supplies

Q: What do you make of that?

Let's make a list of the benefits and downsides to being single.

Q: Which benefits of singleness are the most appealing to you?

• What makes them attractive?

Q: What seems like the biggest downside to being single?

Explain: **Paul continues this thread in verses 32-35 in chapter 7. Let's take a look.**

Q: (If this applies) How has your relationship with God differed during times you were dating as opposed to times when you weren't dating?

Explain: **The point of this discussion is not to say you shouldn't get married, or that singleness is more spiritual. The point is to say that singleness is honorable. It's not written anywhere that you *have* to get married. And as we talk about relationships, I hope you'll come to see that it's possible to have deep, meaningful friendships that are intimate without being sexual.**

> My Savior was a single adult. Go figure.

Q: What does it do to your impression of Jesus if you think of him as a single adult?

Q: If you could plan out your life, would you want to remain single until you're 21, 25, or 30 years old—or even stay that way forever? Why?

Q: Do you have any sense about what God may have in mind for you as a married person or as a single person?

HOW | Will You Go Out with Me? (10 minutes)

The Big Idea: It's hard for some people to ask someone out. It's hard for others to gracefully decline an invitation.

Explain: **It's hard for some people to ask someone out. It's hard for others to gracefully decline an invitation.** This might be a nice time to lead with a personal story of abject—or comic—failure at asking someone out or being asked out.

You'll need—
• Copies of the *Will You Go Out with Me?* handout (on DVD) or Student Journal (**page 73**)
• Pencils

Distribute the *Will You Go Out with Me?* handout and talk through the questions together.

Conclude this element by asking each person to thank God for one good thing about someone in the room—without saying anything that would identify who they're talking about. Welcome them to give thanks for something good about more than one person, if they wish, as long as they remember to protect the identity of the people.

When you sense the time is right, offer your own closing prayer.

HOW I Breaking Up (Is So Very Hard to Do) (10 minutes)

The Big Idea: Breaking up is generally awkward and painful for at least one person. Maybe we can help each other out a bit.

Go first: Bump up the trust level by telling a story about one of your own romantic breakups or the breakup of someone you care for.

> You'll need—
> • Nothing but this Leader's Guide

Q: Without embarrassing anyone (other than yourself), what's your worst breakup story?

Q: What do you think it takes for a breakup to go well?

• What do you think is the biggest barrier to that happening?

Q: If you've gone through a breakup, on a scale of 1 (not even close) to 10 (right on par), how painful was it compared to the greatest emotional pain you've ever felt?

Q: Did you go a little nuts after your breakup? Raise your hand if any of these apply:
- I gained weight.
- I drank heavily.
- I rebounded into an unhealthy relationship.
- I felt suicidal.
- I lost weight.
- I started biting my nails.
- I got into fights.
- I had trouble sleeping.
- I slept too much.
- I felt sexually compulsive.
- I had trouble concentrating.
- I had trouble with my grades.
- I had angry blowups.
- I isolated myself from others.
- I hated being alone, so I constantly surrounded myself with people.

Q: What did it take for you to come out on the other side?

- How long did that take?

- Who contributed to your recovery?

- Where do you think God was in all that? How did that make you feel?

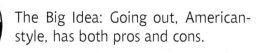

HOW I Kiss Dating Goodbye? (25 minutes)

The Big Idea: Going out, American-style, has both pros and cons.

Team 1: Christians should never date. There should be no physical expression of affection before a couple is engaged to be married.

Team 2: It's fine for Christians to date (especially other Christians). Physical expression of intimacy is perfectly normal and healthy.

Each team will have three minutes to make its case, followed by a two-minute challenge from the other team and a one-minute response.

Explain: **Some people believe there's no room for even the mildest expression of erotic love before people are engaged to be married. That means no dating in the contemporary sense.**

You'll need—
• Copies of the *Kiss Dating Goodbye?* handout (on DVD) or Student Journal (**page 77**)
• Pencils
• List-making supplies
• In advance pick (up to) six opinionated and expressive students (actors and speech + debate competitors are good choices, if you have them) and ask them to defend a position vigorously (whether or not it's what they really think and believe).

In this view you'd remain friends with someone, getting to know that person better and better, but not getting involved physically.

On the other side of this argument, some people believe ordinary dating is the best way for a couple to prepare for marriage and a lifetime commitment to each other.

Here to debate this issue are several people who need no introduction.

Each team will have three minutes to make its case. The other team will have two minutes to challenge that position. The presenting team will have one minute to respond.

We'll follow the example of the apostles in Acts 1:21-26 (not to mention the National Football League) and ask God to tell us which team should go first by the flip of a coin.

After the smoke clears, ask:

Q: How would you summarize the points of view presented here?

Q: Was the way you think about dating challenged in any way?

Distribute the *Kiss Dating Goodbye?* handout and talk through the questions together.

When you reach the end of the handout...

Conclude this element by inviting your group to make a list of things that could make *normal* dating more agreeable for people who are trying to love God with all their heart, soul, mind, and strength and trying to love their neighbors as themselves.

When the list seems as complete as you can make it, invite people to come to the list and put their initials next to the things they want God to help them with.

End with a prayer for grace and endurance to grow through the turmoil of relationships.

SESSION 4

SESSION FOUR | DESIRE

For Your Own Preparation

Desire is good. Except when it's bad.

Healthy desire generates commitment and propels accomplishment. Desire drives one person to sacrifice herself in pursuit of a cure for AIDS. Desire drives another person to indulge in behavior that spreads HIV.

Unhealthy desire, on the other hand (and there's always that dreaded *other hand*), fuels lust.

Desire is so easily twisted:
"I like it," becomes "I want it."
"I want it," becomes "I need it."
"I need it," becomes "You owe it to me."
Which becomes "Never mind, I'll just take it."

> Then, after desire has conceived, it gives birth to sin; and sin, when it is full-grown, gives birth to death. —James 1:15

It's not hard to see what unhealthy desire does to relationships. Look for telltale signs in your students:

— Kids get selfish and pushy when the one thing they desire is the very thing (or experience, or relationship) they can't have. Watch for aggressive or obnoxious behavior (not belligerent, necessarily, but disagreeable nonetheless).

— Those who feel they're entitled to more than they're getting start taking more than they give. Watch for foot-dragging, tardiness, incomplete follow-through, testing limits, whining, and other passive resistance. Listen for reports from their friends of loyalty tests, tongue-lashings, and ultimatums.

— When kids feel something is being withheld from them, they get sneaky and secretive. Look for lying, cover-ups, and burning bridges.

And look for someone on the other side of the relationship who says (sooner than later, we hope), "Who needs that? I'm outta here."

This is a critical moment. The young man or woman with the courage to withdraw from someone whose desire is out of control needs support and encouragement. That person's commitment to health will almost certainly be tested.

> The world breaks everyone and afterward many are strong at the broken places.
> — Ernest Hemingway, *A Farewell to Arms*
>
> Ernest Hemingway, *A Farewell to Arms* (New York: Scribner's and Sons, 1957), p. 249.

The one struggling with unhealthy desire also needs care. Because the next stop may be isolation, followed by obsession, maybe even perversion. If you detect signs of obsession—telephone hang-ups, stalking, self-mutilation—consider a referral to a counselor or school vice principal.

Some people are surprised to learn how many of us expect to struggle with unhealthy desire until we die. That's probably because Christians haven't been talking about that kind of thing lately. But they used to.

> A human being has a natural desire to have more of a good thing than he needs.
> — Mark Twain, *Following the Equator*
>
> Mark Twain, *Following the Equator*, Project Gutenberg EBook edition, 2006, chap. 14

The apostle Paul told his flock in Corinth that God used some kind of persistent problem (he didn't give details) to keep him from being conceited. Paul says he pleaded with God to take it away again and again but God said, "My grace is sufficient for you, for my power is made perfect in weakness" (2 Corinthians 12:9). So, Paul said he came to delight in weakness. He's in a fairly small club—because of his delight, not his weakness.

Some interpretations hold that Paul was referring to some kind of physical weakness, like progressive blindness, and maybe that's right. But lay this passage next to Paul's lament in Romans 7 and see what you get:

So I find this law at work: When I want to do good, evil is right there with me. For in my inner being I delight in God's law; but I see another law at work in the members of my body, waging war against the law of my mind and making me a prisoner of the law of sin at work within my members. What a wretched man I am! Who will rescue me from this body of death? Thanks be to God—through Jesus Christ our Lord!
— Romans 7:21-25, NIV

Some interpretations explain this away; they say Paul is talking about life before he was a Christian. But the evidence suggests another possibility. It's possible that Paul struggled with an unhealthy desire so powerful only God's grace could overcome it. If that's true, then Paul wasn't alone in his struggle with desire, and the rest of us shouldn't be surprised when we struggle. Because desire is tricky that way...

Suggested Session Outline

Other Resources for Teaching on Desire

Reflect for a Moment

We can't lead students where we're not willing to go ourselves. We can point them... but they'd rather be guided. Here are a few questions to consider as you prepare to lead this session on desire.

Q: What has been your most positive experience with healthy desire?

• What made it so positive?

Q: What has been your most negative experience with unhealthy desire?

• Is that resolved? If so, how did you get resolution? If not, how would you describe your current situation?

Q: What do you think it would cost you to be open with at least one safe person about your struggle with unhealthy desire? Do you think you can afford that risk?

Q: If you had just one hour to talk with kids about desire, what would you try to communicate?

• Why do you think that's so important?

• If you were prevented from lecturing on the subject, how would you try to communicate during that hour?

NOW | Guess Who Is Sexually Active (20 minutes)

The Big Idea: Surprise, surprise, we're all "sexually active," with desires that are often good, and sometimes bad, but rarely indifferent.

Welcome your group: **It's great to see you. I have some big news for you all today. It has recently come to my attention that several members of this group are sexually active. I don't want to freak anybody out, but I've decided to name them in public right now.** (Pause as the room becomes silent, with every eye riveted on you.) **I've learned that everyone in this room—100 percent—is sexually active.**

Now would be a good time to smile.

Continue: **Okay, relax, I don't know anything you hope I don't know. I'm just saying there's no such thing as a sexually inactive teenager because all teenagers deal with the opposite gender, their own bubbling hormones, and more or less intense sexual desires. All teenagers everywhere are sexually active in the sense that you're growing and making choices about what to do sexually.**

Q: Do you agree with that statement? Why or why not?

Q: How does this compare with what most people seem to mean when they talk about teens being "sexually active"?

Q: A few new terms have popped up in our culture in the last several years: "friends with benefits" and "hook-ups." What do these terms mean? Given that

You'll need—
• A television or video projection unit
• A DVD player
• The *Good Sex* DVD, cued to "Desire"
• Copies of the *Guess Who Is Sexually Active* handout (on DVD) or Student Journal (**page 82**)
• Pencils

I hate it when adults use the term "sexually active." What does that even mean? Am I gonna like deactivate someday, or is it a permanent state of being?
— Juno MacGuff, in *Juno* (Fox Searchlight Pictures, 2007)

FYI: About 63 percent of high school students who've had sexual intercourse during a three-month period in 2005 report using condoms. That's up from 46 percent in 1991.

Federal Interagency Forum on Child and Family Statistics, *America's Children: Key National Indicators of Well-Being, 2007.* (Washington, DC: U.S. Government Printing Office).

these terms are new, do you think that means the sexual desires of teenagers and young adults are increasing or not?

Q: Boys' average age of *spermarche* (the first time a boy ejaculates sperm) is about 14, and girls' average age of *menarche* (a girl's first menstruation) is now at about age 13. Boys' average age of marriage is just over 26, and girls' average age of marriage is around 24. How do you think the gap between the hormonal onset of puberty and the average age of marriage relates to our sexual desire?

Explain: **I want to play you a video clip on desire and then chat about it.**

After the video is finished, ask—

Q: Is sexual desire a good or a bad thing?

• Why do you think that?

• When can it be a good thing?

• When can it be a bad thing?

Instead of playing the DVD, with a little preparation, you can have students perform "Desire." The video transcript is on the DVD.

A common theme among teens is that their sexual desire is *so* strong, they just can't stop themselves. Is it so strong that if their parents walked in on what they were doing, they still wouldn't be able to stop?

Q: George Bernard Shaw wrote: "There are two tragedies in life. One is not to get your heart's desire. The other is to get it."[19] Do you think this is true or not? Can you give any examples from your own life to support your opinion?

Explain: **Imagine that we define desire as "something to long for, a craving, a wish." But this isn't the only force that drives us. There's something else that we call "need." The dictionary says that need is "a necessity, a lack of something required." It's that thing that we just cannot do without; if we don't get it, we die.**

Q: If I were to walk around your school and ask whether sexual fulfillment is a desire or a need, what would kids say?

19. George Bernard Shaw, *Man and Superman* (1903), act 4.

• What do you think?

Explain: **The video ends with a desire that maybe you haven't thought of before: That God would transform what we really need into what we really want. Today we're going to figure out together what in the world that means.**

To help students reflect futher on their own sexual desires, use the material included on the *Guess Who Is Sexually Active* handout (on DVD), or Student Journal **page 82**, for large group discussion, small group time, or as a tool for individual personal reflection.

NEW | Sweet Dreams Are Made of This (25 minutes)

The Big Idea: Both Jesus and the apostle Paul offer us straight talk about lust and what to do about it.

Read the following to your students:

Betsy, Reggie, and Juanita live on the same block and go to the same school. Back in the day, they used to ride bikes together in the neighborhood, but now they've drifted apart. They're into different things at school and have totally different friends now, so they barely say hi anymore when they bump into each other between classes or at lunch.

You'll need—
• Bibles

But if you could look into their rooms after school, you'd see they still have a lot in common.

Betsy sits in her bedroom watching soaps on the TV she talked her parents into buying for her birthday. The people on the screen are undressing each other (though Betsy doesn't actually see them naked), and in the next shot they're under the covers and there's no doubt what they're doing. Betsy's eyes, ears, and emotions are riveted to the screen.

Reggie grabs chips and a Doctor Pepper, ducks a homework question from his mom, and heads up to his room. He pulls a sports magazine from the lining of his gym bag, but this issue has less to do with baseball and more to do with swimwear—if you catch my drift. He locks the door, flops down on the bed, and opens the magazine.

Juanita sits on her bed listening to the radio. She can't stop thinking about her conversation with Omar. He is impossibly cute and seemed really interested in what she was doing after school. She wonders what it would be like to go out with him. She closes her eyes and imagines him coming over. She sees herself opening the door and it's Omar, in an oversized sweater and jeans. "Hey," he says, lifting his chin the tiniest bit as he speaks. And a faint smile dances around his eyes.

Q: Do you think Betsy is lusting? Explain your answer.

- Do you think Reggie is lusting? Why?

- What about Juanita—do you think she's lusting? Why?

Q: Do you think there's a difference between lusting and merely daydreaming? If so, what is it?

Now read Matthew 5:27-30 together.

Q: What do you think Jesus is getting at here?

- What would you say is Jesus' definition of adultery?

Explain: **In Matthew 5:27, Jesus quotes Exodus 20:14, but his real goal was to show the true meaning of the commandment against adultery. As he often did, Jesus focuses here on people's hearts, not just their actions. He defines lust as imagining a forbidden sexual relationship. I doubt Jesus literally wants every person to gouge out an eye or cut off a hand if it causes them to sin. We'd all be shy some body parts in that case. He wants to show that lust is such a radical sin that it requires a radical response. The people who first heard his words would have a shared cultural belief that the right eye and right hand were more valuable than the left, making the consequences of lust even more extreme.**

FYI: According to a 2007 study of college students, conducted by the University of Texas, the top three reasons male and female collegiates said they had sex were the same: They were attracted to the other person, it feels good, and they wanted to experience physical pleasure.

Q: What do you think about this? Why?

Q: Let's ask the questions again. *Do you think Betsy was lusting? Why?*

- *Do you think Reggie was lusting? Why?*

- *Do you think Juanita was lusting? Why?*

Q: When does daydreaming turn to lust?

Q: Do you have any experience with daydreams turning to lust? If so, how do you think it happened?

Q: Do you identify with any of these three characters? Why?

Explain: **I'm going to read some Scripture passages written by the apostle Paul, and I want you to think about how they each relate to the characters (Betsy, Reggie, Juanita)—and to you.**

Read Romans 6:11-13 aloud.

Q: The verb tense of "do not let sin reign" in Romans 6:12 is the present tense, implying that it's a daily and ongoing decision to offer the parts of our bodies to God, instead of sin. Paul offers no middle ground between offering ourselves to God and offering ourselves to sin. What would "do not let sin reign" mean for the character most like you in the stories we read?

One time (actually a series of times) I tried to deal with a sexual temptation by pledging to give $100 to missions every time I gave in. Well, not only did I give in, but I also failed to follow through with my pledge—no single missions organization got any richer. I wish I'd just lived out Colossians 3:1-5 instead.
— KP

Q: How would the character with whom you most closely identify offer the parts of his or her body to righteousness?

Now read 1 Thessalonians 4:3-5.

Q: Paul describes a difference between people who know God and those who don't. Why does God care about how Betsy, Reggie, and Juanita respond to their sexual desires?

Q: If Betsy, Reggie, or Juanita wanted to learn from someone else what it means to control your own body, what examples might they turn to?

Finally, read Colossians 3:5 out loud.

Q: Any time there is a *therefore,* we have to look to previous sentences, so we really need to read Colossians 3:1-4 also. Many of the verbs in this passage describe what believers already are—they have *died,* they have been *raised* with Christ, their lives are now *hidden* in Christ. But another verb is used twice to describe what believers should then be able to do, namely *set* their hearts on things above. Okay, forget about Betsy, Reggie, and Juanita and answer for yourself (if you haven't already begun to do so): What do *you* think it means for you to have died with Christ?

• How do you think setting your heart on things above might affect your sexual imagination?

Q: If you could live in the reality of Colossians 3:1-5, what, if anything, would change in your life?

HOW | Sisterhood of the Traveling Hormones (20 minutes)

The Big Idea: In the midst of our desires, we can find escape routes that glorify God.

You'll need—
• A copy of the movie *The Sisterhood of the Traveling Pants* (Warner Bros., 2005), cued to scene 21 (01:03:00)
• A television or video projection unit
• A DVD player
• Copies of the *Escape Route* handout (on DVD)
• Pencils

FYI: We're not endorsing everything in this movie, we're just saying this clip is useful. If that makes you (or your boss) uncomfortable, then let your conscience be your guide.

Prepare to show a video clip from *The Sisterhood of the Traveling Pants*. In this scene Bridget (played by Blake Lively) describes her overwhelming desire for Eric (played by Mike Vogel), even though he's off-limits because he's her coach at soccer camp.

Set the scene for the clip by explaining that, in the movie, four high school best friends who are away for the summer decide to stay in touch through letters. And in this scene Bridget describes her romantic feelings for her soccer coach. Play the scene, stopping the video just over three minutes later after Bridget says, "Come on, I'll race you."

(Note: Approximately two-and-a-half minutes into the scene, Eric says, "You scare the hell out of me." If that phrase is inappropriate in your context, feel free to stop the DVD just as Bridget is walking onto the beach.)

Q: In her letter Bridget confesses, "What can I say? I'm obsessed, and as we all know, obsessed girls cannot be responsible for our actions." What do you think about that?

Q: Based on what you know about lust, do you think Bridget was lusting?

Q: In our culture, we tend to think guys have stronger sexual desires than girls do. Is that more wrong than right, or more right than wrong?

Q: How, if at all, do you think the fact that Bridget's mom died has affected her level of sexual desire?

Q: Note how uncomfortable Eric feels about Bridget's advances on the beach. If you could look inside his mind and see his thoughts, what do you think they would be? *(Skip this question if you cut before the beach scene.)*

Q: Why do you think Bridget ends their conversation abruptly and says, "I'll race you"? *(Also skip this question if you cut before the beach scene.)*

Q: When you're faced with sexual temptation, like Eric and Bridget both are, what are the things you tend to tell yourself?

• Which of these are helpful? Which are dangerous?

• If your little sister asked you the one thing she should remember when she gets heated up sexually, what would you tell her? Why that?

Read 1 Corinthians 10:13.

Q: What stands out for you in this verse?

• Why do you think that's important?

Q: What does this verse say about God?

Q: Teenagers often think they "can't help" having sex. How does Paul's writing relate to that theme?

• What difference do you think that could make in your life with your own desires?

Conclude by giving students time to pray in pairs or small groups, asking God to help them experience God's faithfulness and escape routes in the midst of their sexual desires.

Further questions for students' individual personal reflection can be found on the *Escape Route* handout (on DVD).

FYI: When asked "Do you think that people should wait to have sex until they are married, or not necessarily?" more than 7 out of 10 evangelical Protestant teenagers responded, "yes," topped only by Mormons at 77 percent. Approximately 50 percent of Mainline Protestant and Roman Catholic teenagers also agreed.

Mark Regnerus, *Forbidden Fruit* (New York: Oxford University Press, 2007), p. 86.

FYI: A common theme in the interviews of the National Study of Youth and Religion was that students "can't help" having sex. A second theme was that students think sex is okay once they're "emotionally ready" for it.

Other Resources for Teaching on Desire

NOW | SexTalk: Desire (20 minutes)

The Big Idea: We all face desire, but we don't face it alone.

Play the "SexTalk: Desire" segment. After the video ends, ask—

Q: What was the most interesting phrase or idea mentioned in this video?

• What made it so interesting?

Q: Why is it that we often view teenage sexual desire as a bad thing?

• How do you think God views teenage sexual desire?

Q: The video says, "Whatever you can't get enough of, that's your god." Do you agree or disagree? Talk about that.

At this point distribute pencils and the *SexTalk: Desire* handout (on DVD), giving students plenty of time to reflect and respond personally.

You'll need—
• A television or video projection unit
• A DVD player
• The *Good Sex* DVD, cued to "SexTalk: Desire"
• Copies of the *SexTalk: Desire* handout (on DVD) or Student Journal (**page 83**)
• Pencils

Instead of playing the DVD, with a little preparation, you can have a student perform "SexTalk: Desire" as a monologue. The video transcript is on the DVD.

NOW | The Nature of Desire (15 mins)

The Big Idea: Sexual desires come in many forms.

Explain: **As you might have realized already, sexual desire has many faces. What can be an incredible temptation to commit sexual sin for one person could be a thing that someone else would just laugh off or find disgusting. Have a listen to a few of these stories.** At this point, read the stories aloud yourself.

> You'll need—
> • Zip, nada, nothing (other than this book, of course)

STORY 1

Brian has a friend named Cory. They've been friends for years now and have spent a lot of time at each other's houses. Brian particularly loves to go to Cory's house for one reason: Cory's older sister is unbelievably good-looking. For years Brian has had sexual fantasies about his best friend's sister, but lately things have been getting worse.

Just the other day, Brian had an uncontrollable urge to sneak into Cory's sister's bedroom and go through her underwear drawer. He had no idea why he was doing it, he knew that it made no sense, but something drew him into her bedroom. Just as he was going through her underwear, Cory walked into the bedroom and caught Brian. Their relationship is over now, and even worse for Brian is the shame of having to go to school every day, knowing that everybody knows what he was caught doing.

*(NOTE: It seems that Brian might be edging into fetishism. For more information on sexual fetishes, see "A Note about Sexual Fetishes" at the end of this session on **page 150**.)*

STORY 2

Jackie has a reputation at school. She doesn't know why she does it, but she just can't get enough. Every time she goes out with a guy on a date, the desire to perform oral sex or to receive it overwhelms her. It's gotten to the point now where if at the end of a date she does not either perform this act or have it done to her, she views it as a wasted night.

She cannot stand the way the other girls talk about her at school, but this desire has a hold on her life. She only feels complete as a sexual person when she's giving in to this sexual desire.

STORY 3

Josh has been going to church with his family for as long as he can remember. His mom is pretty strict; she doesn't let him see any movies that are PG-13, let alone R. She refuses to get cable for the house because she doesn't approve of the kind of TV shows that are shown on those other networks.

> Much of today's pornography portrays women in submissive positions and men as sexual aggressors.
>
> Mark Regnerus, *Forbidden Fruit* (New York: Oxford University Press, 2007), p. 179.

Josh doesn't mind too much because, frankly, his best friend Austin has cable TV, so Josh can watch whatever he wants to when he's over there. Plus Austin has all sorts of movie stations, so any movie that Josh missed in the theatre he can catch a few months later.

One day before the summer of their ninth-grade year, Josh and Austin were hanging out as usual, watching TV, when Austin said, "Hey, Josh, shut the door." Austin turned on his laptop and went to a porn Web site. Josh had never seen pictures like that before, and he was intrigued. He and Austin stared at them for more than a half-hour. They did the same the next day, and the day after that, and the day after that. Austin gave Josh his list of favorite porn sites, and whenever Josh had more than 10 minutes to himself in his room, he'd flip on his computer and just stare at the beautiful and exotic women. He couldn't get enough of them.

Q: Do you know anyone who seems to be driven the way Brian, Jackie, and Josh are driven? Without embarrassing anyone or naming names, can you tell us what you know about that person's struggle?

Q: If any of them came to you seeking advice for a way to control these sexual desires, what advice would you give?

Q: Some would say it's not possible to control our sexual desires. What do you think?

Q: It's been said that thanks to the Internet, teenagers who wish to avoid pornography have to go out of their way to do so. What do you think about that?

Q: In one survey, 71 percent of 18-to-24-year-olds report seeing more pornography online than offline (in other words, in magazines, movie theatres, and on TV).[20] Based on what you know about teenagers, what percentage do you think see more pornography online than offline?

Transition to the next step by explaining: **While for Brian, Jackie, Josh, and maybe some of you, sexual desires can seem overwhelming, the Scriptures give us some specific ideas that can help us.**

---

20. Pamela Paul, *Pornified: How Pornography Is Transforming Our Lives, Our Relationships, and Our Families* (New York: Times Books, 2005), p. 172.

NOW | Behind the Scenes (20 mins)

The Big Idea: Behind the scenes, desires often drive what we do and say.

Explain: **Today we're going to start by looking behind the scenes at Jessica and Mario on a date.**

You'll need—
• Four student volunteers
• Four copies of *Behind the Scenes Drama* (on DVD)
• Copies of the *Behind the Scenes* handout (on DVD) or Student Journal (**page 84**)
• Pencils
• In advance recruit four student volunteers and have them arrive early enough to read over the *Behind the Scenes Drama* script ahead of time. They don't have to memorize their lines, but they should be familiar enough to read through them easily. Set up four chairs—two rows of two. Lower the lights if you can, to add to the mood.

Read "The Setting" on the *Behind the Scenes* script to launch the drama.

As the sketch ends and the lights come back on, invite a warm round of applause for your sure-to-be-Oscar-Award-winning cast, and then ask the following questions.

Q: We don't know for sure what happened next for Jessica and Mario. What do you think happened? Why do you think that?

Q: Do you think people ever go through what Jessica and Mario went through? Talk about that.

• How about you? Have you ever had that kind of experience? Can you talk about it?

Q: How are Jessica's and Mario's inner voices similar?

• How are they different?

Q: What habits and attitudes do you think lie behind Jessica's and Mario's actions? I'll read a list; you tell me which ones you think fit and why.

• Anxiety   because...

• Desire   because...

- Fear   because...

- Honesty   because...

- Hope   because...

- Lust   because...

- Manipulation because...

- Old patterns because...

- Possessiveness because...

- Pride   because...

- Self-examination because...

- Sneakiness   because...

Q: Do you think these fears, anxieties, and desires are different for people who don't call themselves Christians and people who do?

To conclude this part of the discussion, distribute copies of the *Behind the Scenes* handout (on DVD), or Student Journal (**page 84**), and ask students to individually reflect and journal about their own experiences, desires, and motivations. Invite students to think about (or even jot down) what they'd like to talk about with the person they listed at the bottom of the handout as you continue with the rest of your meeting.

NEW | Hang Onto Your Hormones (15 mins)

The Big Idea: Controlling our desires comes with both costs and advantages.

Read the following story about a student who wrestled with her sexual desires.

You'll need—
- Bibles

Every Tuesday and Thursday after swim team practice, I went to Max's house, just to hang out. Max's mom worked long hours, so once his older brother went away to college, Max spent most afternoons at home alone. He did homework, watched television, went online, and talked every day to his girlfriend, Ginny, when she had a break from her after-school job at the video store. Ginny didn't mind that Max and I hung out because Ginny and I had been friends since the fifth grade.

Max started telling me about all the problems he and Ginny were having. Ginny worked so much that they never had any time together. And when they did have time together, she was always so tired that she never felt like doing anything. Even though they talked on the phone every day, Max was getting tired of having a girlfriend he never saw.

One Thursday, Max was especially angry. He told me all the details of how Ginny had just called to tell him she couldn't go out with him on Friday night because—guess what—she had to work.

Max told me, "I just wish Ginny was a little more like you and had some more time for me."

I started getting a little uncomfortable with Max's compliments, so I went to the bathroom. When I came out I noticed that Max had turned down all the lights. Max wanted me to sit next to him on the couch, which was where we normally sat when we watched TV. But for some reason, it felt different this time. Maybe because the television wasn't on, but I wasn't sure.

Max put his hand on my hand. I wanted to move my hand, but to be honest, Max's hand felt pretty good. Max leaned against me, putting his head on my shoulder. The lights were dim, and I was starting to really like how Max's head felt on my shoulder.

After a few minutes, Max started to touch my ear, and then my cheek. I was torn. I knew I should stop him, but it felt so good. Max leaned forward and kissed me on my cheek, and then he moved his lips toward mine...

Q: What do you think she'll do? Why?

Transition to Scripture by explaining: **Someone not too much older than that girl—or you, for that matter—was faced with a similar situation.**

Read Genesis 39:1-23 with your students. *(Consider asking several students to read different sections for the group.)* Use the following questions for discussion.

Q: What do you like best about this story? Why?

Explain: **Joseph must have been pretty good-looking because the Bible, which seldom refers to physical appearances, describes him in Genesis 39:6 as "well-built and handsome." It must have run in the family—the only other person in the Old Testament praised for both her figure and face was Joseph's mom, Rachel, who was described in Genesis 29:17 as having "a lovely figure and...beautiful."**

> FYI: Genesis 39:2 gives the overall theme for the story: "The Lord was with Joseph so that he prospered." The story of Joseph is not so much about Joseph's success as it is God's faithfulness to his people and God's promises.

Q: Given that, put yourself in Joseph's place. You're a talented, good-looking slave kid who would, no doubt, like to hang onto your job—not to mention your head. What would you guess you'd think and feel if your owner's wife came on to you?

Q: Are you surprised by Joseph's choices?

Q: Put yourself in Mrs. Potiphar's place. How do you think you'd feel if the good-looking slave kid turned down your generous offer of sex?

Q: Put yourself in Mr. Potiphar's place. How do you think you'd feel if you came home to find your wife in hysterics, holding the clothes of the good-looking slave kid and claiming he tried to rape her?

Explain: **In prison Joseph eventually meets people who connect him with the pharaoh. Seeing how talented Joseph is (and it doesn't hurt that God gives Joseph insight into God's plans for Egypt), the pharaoh places Joseph in charge of the government, and Joseph prepares the whole nation to survive a drought that devastates the rest of the world. I wonder what would have happened if Joseph hadn't refused to have sex with Potiphar's wife...**

Q: Do you see any similarities between the story of Joseph and the story we read earlier?

Q: Put yourself in the shoes of the person telling the story that we read before. What are the possible consequences—good and bad—if you decline to give in to Max's advances? Be as specific as you can.

Q: What are some possible consequences—good and bad—if you give Max (and actually *yourself*) what he wants? Be specific.

Transition to the next step by explaining: **Next we're going to discuss how the story of the swimmer and the story of Joseph relate to our own personal stories and our own personal responses to our sexual desires.**

NEW | Is Masturbation Okay? (20 mins)

The Big Idea: God's Word and God's community can help us experience freedom from sexual behaviors that can become addictive.

Explain: **Okay, so you've heard the word *masturbation* and maybe even joked about it with others in the school locker room. But do you really know what it is? And have you come to terms with what God might say about it and how God's opinion relates to your own behaviors?**

Let's take one question at a time.

First, *What is masturbation?* That's probably the easiest one of all. It's touching your own genital organs to stimulate yourself and have a sexual experience.

> You'll need—
> • Bibles
> • Whiteboard or poster paper
> • Pens
> • Copies of the *Is Masturbation Okay?* handout (on DVD) or Student Journal (**page 85**)
> • Pencils

Next, *What does God say about it?* Well, the word *masturbation* never appears in the Bible.

• Some Christians think masturbation is always wrong because (1) it often involves fantasizing about someone sexually, and (2) it's a form of sexual stimulation, which they believe should be saved for marriage.

• Some Christians think masturbation is perfectly all right and a normal way to release sexual pressures.

• Some Christians fall somewhere in the middle, saying masturbation may be okay, but it can easily become addictive and controlling, so do it only rarely.

One of the issues is that lots of people find that once they start masturbating, they can't stop. Ron had that problem. He had started masturbating in ninth grade, both because of his own curiosity and because it felt good. He did it more often in tenth grade, and pretty much every night in eleventh grade. Now that he's a senior, he's realizing it's starting to control him, and he wants to stop.

Well, at least part of him wants to stop. Another part of him enjoys it way too much and wants to do it even more.

So Ron is really confused. He's tried everything he's heard of that might help—taking showers, exercising, avoiding any pictures of girls that might get him thinking about sex—but he still feels trapped.

Q: What would you say to Ron if he asked you what he should do?

Continue: **Although the Bible never uses the word *masturbation*, it gives us all sorts of principles that help us know what we should do. Let's start with 1 Corinthians 10:13—"No temptation has overtaken you except what is common to us all. And God is faithful; he will not let you be tempted beyond what you can bear. But when you are tempted, he will also provide a way out so that you can endure it."**

Q: How does 1 Corinthians 10:13 relate to obsessive or compulsive masturbation?

Q: Now let's look at James 1:13-15. How do you think masturbation could become a temptation that results in sin?

• Do you think it's possible to masturbate only occasionally, unlike Ron who found that it became more addictive?

At this point draw a circle on your whiteboard, and at the top of the circle, write the word *Fantasy*, like so:

FYI: According to Dr. Mark Laaser, there are three common "building blocks" that lead to sexual addictions: sexual fantasizing, masturbation, and use of pornography. They work together and reinforce each other; pornography stimulates fantasy, and masturbation allows for an expression of a fantasy.

Mark Laaser, *Faithful and True: Sexual Integrity in a Fallen World* (Grand Rapids, Mich.: Zondervan, 1996), pp. 25–29.

FYI: Temptation cannot come from God because God's nature doesn't allow it. Instead, the source of temptation lies within us as humans.

STEP 1: FANTASY

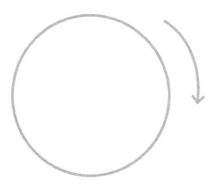

Explain that many of our sexual behaviors, including masturbation, start with fantasy.

Draw the second step of the circle, which is "Acting Out." It's at this point that a person like Ron is likely to masturbate.

STEP 1: FANTASY

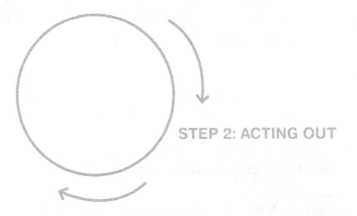

STEP 2: ACTING OUT

Q: How does Ron tend to feel after he's acted out sexually? Answers will likely vary from "good" to "ashamed." At this point, draw the third step of the circle, which is "Isolation."

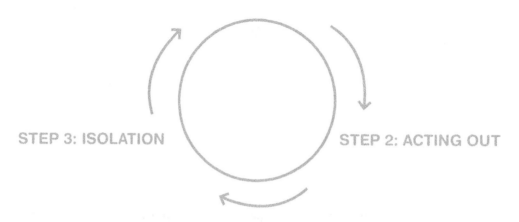

STEP 1: FANTASY

STEP 3: ISOLATION

STEP 2: ACTING OUT

Q: Based on the isolation that Ron feels, what's he likely to do?

Q: Some refer to the circle we've just drawn as a "Cycle of Addiction." Why do you think they call it that?

Q: It's been suggested that the circle can also work in the reverse; that addiction can start with isolation (as well as other emotions), and then move toward acting out and fantasizing. Do you agree or disagree?

Q: Looking at this Cycle of Addiction can make someone struggling with sexual addiction feel rather hopeless, like there's no way she can escape. What would you want to say to someone who feels that way?

• Based on what you know about Jesus, what do you think Jesus would say to someone who feels like she can't escape her addictions?

Q: Okay, now let's get more personal. Forget Ron. How, if at all, do 1 Corinthians 10:13 and James 1:13-15 relate to the circle we've just drawn?

Q: How do you think God would want you to act when it comes to masturbation?

• Do you think it's possible that God thinks masturbation is okay? If so, why do you think that? When might it become not okay?

• Do you think it's possible that God would want us to avoid masturbation at all times? If so, why do you think that?

At this point, distribute pencils and copies of the *Is Masturbation Okay?* handout to your students, giving them plenty of time to reflect and respond.

HOW | Until I Get Married (15 mins)

STEP 3: HOW

The Big Idea: There are long-term consequences that come from unhealthy responses to our sexual desires.

You'll need—
- Copies of the *Until I Get Married* handout (on DVD) or Student Journal (**page 88**)
- Pencils
- A married adult volunteer
- In advance ask a married member of your adult volunteer team (maybe even you) to share about his or her premarital sexual experiences, how those experiences relate to desire before being married, and how that has affected his or her marriage so far. (This can be someone who has regrets or someone who doesn't.)

FYI: Multiple studies confirm that even if students regret their first sexual experience, few stop there. Only about 10 percent of non-virgins have had sex only one time.

Mark Regnerus, *Forbidden Fruit* (New York: Oxford University Press, 2007), p. 132.

Explain: **The majority of people who want to get married eventually do. And when they get married, they bring their past sexual experiences into the marriage with them. Some of you have already had sexual experiences, either by your own choice or not (as in cases of sexual abuse). Some of you regret what you've experienced already. Others want to experience even more as quickly as possible.**

Since I can't be with you every time you make a decision in response to your sexual desires, my job is to prepare you ahead of time, if possible. So I've asked a friend to tell his (or her) story. I'll try to give you a chance to ask questions when he's (or she's) done.

At this point, introduce your friend and have him or her tell the story. When he or she is finished, ask—

Q: What's the most important thing that you heard in that story?

- Why is that important to you?

Q: What difference could this true story make in the way you live out your sexual desires? Why?

Q: If you had the chance to ask our friend a follow-up question, what would that be?

Q: Lots of young people tend to think that sex "just happens." Do you agree, or do you think it's more like a choice you make? Explain your answer.

To help your students respond more personally and think about the sexual choices they'd like to make, distribute copies of the *Until I Get Married* handout and pencils. Then give your students time to reflect and journal about their feelings.

Depending on how much time you have, and how vulnerable your students tend to be, you may want to conclude by dividing them into pairs to share a few things they've written and close in prayer.

A Note about Sexual Fetishes

Here and there you'll meet someone with a sexualized obsession toward a nonsexual object or behavior.

I have a friend who is aroused by the sound of spiked-heel shoes on a hard floor. As a boy the fantasy of a woman stepping on his hand became attached to his sexual arousal. He doesn't know why.

Another friend is aroused by women smoking cigarettes. He doesn't think he's alone in this, because he found whole Web sites devoted to images of people smoking. He believes his own fascination grew from his parents' preoccupation with the evils of smoking when he was young. The rule in his house (this was in the 1950s) was they had to turn off the sound when a cigarette commercial came on television. He thinks he got the impression that anything *that* bad might actually be good. (Perhaps this was a trust issue with his parents?)

Another man I know loves women's undergarments. He thinks his appetite for silky things refers back to emotional turmoil from watching his father abuse his mother. His wife told me his lingerie is nicer than hers. It probably goes without saying that it puts a strain on their marriage.

A few people are turned on by causing or receiving or observing pain.

All of these (and quite a few more) are *fetishes*—a term that refers to attaching unwarranted devotion to an object or behavior. There's nothing obviously sexual about these things, yet a few people find them arousing. There may be a student in your group who wrestles with sexual fetishism.

Why do some people have sexual fetishes? I don't know.

My best guess is that fetishism is what Gerald May calls *attraction addiction*.

Attraction addictions are marked by all of the following—
- Tolerance—*I need more and more to get the same results over time.*
- Withdrawal symptoms—*I feel bad if I don't get what I long for.*
- Self-deception—*I lie to myself with excuses, denials, and other mind games.*
- Loss of willpower—*I don't know how to control my longing.*

- Distortion of attention—*My longing interrupts love for God, others, and me.*[21]

If someone you know struggles with a sexual fetish, you can bet that person feels isolated by the obsession. She's probably emotionally, and perhaps physically, exhausted from the energy expended fighting or hiding what she's up to. And she's afraid—though sometimes she longs to talk with someone about her confusion and pain, even if it means being caught. And there's probably another addiction that's more obvious—an addiction to food or making money or spending it or any of a zillion personalized obsessions or compulsions that obscure the fetish. Which is not to say the fetish is necessarily the most destructive obsession that person deals with, but it may produce the most shame because it's the most unusual and the most difficult to admit and talk about.

Because of the characteristics of addiction—tolerance, withdrawal symptoms, self-deception, loss of willpower, distortion of attention—fetishes sometimes lead to increasingly risky, even dangerous, behavior. That's why it's important to try to help people struggling with sexual fetishes.

Which is a challenge in youth groups. Most kids never mention fetishes in youth groups because lots of youth workers make jokes about such things, and who wants to be the butt of jokes? So if you want to serve someone struggling with a sexual fetish, start by not making fun of temptations you don't understand.

To go further, let your group know you're aware that some people struggle with issues they've never heard anybody else talk about. Tell them you're willing to talk in private with anyone who'd like to ask questions about temptation or struggle.

Then be prepared for the possibility that no one will say anything—or someone may tell you they're the victim of sexual assault; or somebody might talk with you about a "friend"; or who knows what else? The important thing is that you express your openness to any conversation.

Having said that, it's important to acknowledge that if someone does talk with you about a sexual fetish, you probably won't know what to do. If that's true, do this—
- Listen compassionately. Ask thoughtful questions. Use the five marks of addiction (above) to explore the strength of the fetish. Take your time.

---

21. Gerald May, *Addiction and Grace: Love and Spirituality in the Healing of Addictions* (New York: Harper-Collins, 1998), p. 37.

- Be honest about the limits of your knowledge and skills.
- Reassure her of your commitment to confidentiality and ask if you may put her in touch with someone who has more experience in this area than you. Offer to go with her. (See **page 259** for some thoughts on referrals.)
- If you don't already know who that other helper is, then find him in a timely manner and follow through with what you promised. If it takes more time than you thought, let your young friend know what's going on so she's not left to wonder. Be aware that she'll probably feel pretty vulnerable during this time because the cat is out of the bag.
- Follow through. Stay in touch. Don't act as if the conversation never happened. Ask thoughtful questions. Keep confidentiality. Pray for her. And guard your own heart.

SESSION 5

SESSION FIVE | BOUNDARIES

For Your Own Preparation

The Bible doesn't even acknowledge the one question that kids ask most often about sex—at least not directly.

The question goes something like this: "I know I'm not supposed to have sex, okay? But how far can I go? I mean, is it okay to get into, you know, scoring position?"

Well...if sex were a game, that would be an interesting question. But sex is less like a game than a super-intimate conversation. Sex is less like a game than a secret, whispered between lovers.

"FINE! Look, I'm just trying to get a little without having God all mad at me! So, for crying out loud, will you please just tell me, HOW FAR CAN I GO?"

Well, okay. But you may not like the answer because the Bible doesn't really talk about sex and dating in any modern sense. What the Bible *does* talk about—quite a bit, actually—is lust.

So here it is: You may go as far as you wish, as long as you stop before you lust.

???

Lust is a serious fixation on something that's not mine to have; it's a deep, focused, inappropriate craving. In the biblical languages, the images associated with lust are heavy breathing, smoldering, and bursting into flames. The Bible doesn't talk about hooking up or friends with benefits; it talks about breaking boundaries to get what isn't mine to take.

This chapter is about learning to identify and respect sexual boundaries.

Reflect for a Moment

We can't lead students where we're not willing to go ourselves. We can point them... but they'd rather be guided. Here are a few questions to consider as you prepare to lead this session on boundaries.

Q: How did you become aware of the need for sexual boundaries in your life?

Q: In what areas do you have the greatest difficulty living within your sexual boundaries?

Q: If you're in a relationship with someone who encourages you to maintain healthy sexual boundaries, reflect on what that person does that's helpful.

• What does that help cost you? Is it worth it?

Q: If you're in a relationship with someone who doesn't encourage you to maintain healthy sexual boundaries, what do you think that may be costing you?

• What do you think it would cost you to find a person who'd encourage you to maintain healthy sexual boundaries? Do you think it would be worth it?

Q: If you had just one hour to talk with kids about sexual boundaries, what would you try to communicate?

• Why do you think that's so important?

• If you were prevented from lecturing on the subject, how would you try to communicate during that hour?

NOW | When Is It Sex? (15 minutes)

The Big Idea: Identifying the sexual boundaries

Play the video, then ask—

You'll need—
• A television or video projection unit
• DVD player
• The *Good Sex* DVD, cued to "When Is It Sex?"
• Copies of the *When Is It Sex?* handout (on DVD) or Student Journal (**page 92**)
• Pencils

Instead of playing the DVD, with a little preparation, you can have students perform "When Is It Sex?" The video transcript is on the DVD.

Q: What stood out to you as spot on or way off base in these responses?

• Did you hear anything surprising or troubling?

Distribute the *When Is It Sex?* handout and walk through it together.

Here are a couple of quotes you can use in the discussion, if you wish:

When you give too much of yourself away too quickly, when you show too much skin, you're not being true to yourself. When you dress to show us everything, then in some sense we have all shared in it, or at least been exposed to it. There is a mystery to you, infinite depth and endless complexity.[22]
— Rob Bell, *Sex God*

Anal sex is one of the most effective ways to transmit an STD. The receptive partner has the highest risk of contracting the disease. HIV, Hepatitis C and all other STDs can also be transmitted this way. And don't forget the wart virus. Most people aren't aware that being exposed to the wart virus and the human papilloma virus (HPV) by contact with the anal region seems to increase the risk for anal cancer....I must say that I'm really quite bewildered by the preoccupation of anal sex and all the questions I get about it these days. I don't know if the pornographic industry has somehow raised awareness of this activity, or if this is some sort of an aggressive act that men are looking

---

22. Rob Bell, *Sex God* (Grand Rapids, Mich.: Zondervan, 2007), p. 124.

to perpetrate against women. Certainly both partners must be willing to do this. Care needs to be taken to not damage the women's anal sphincter or rectum, as this is a part of the body that can be injured. If the woman is not interested in this behavior she should not feel as though she is letting her partner down if she doesn't engage in it. If this is not something you want to do you should not be doing it.[23]

— Dr. Drew Pinsky, "drDrewSpeak: Oral and Anal Sex," DrDrew.com

Transition: **Let's see what happens when Christians behave in ways that are indistinguishable from anyone else.**

---

23. Dr. Drew Pinsky, "drDrewSpeak: Oral and Anal Sex," DrDrew.com, 2001, http://www.drdrew.com/DrewLive/article.asp?id=1294 (accessed July 29, 2008).

NEW | Yes, Master (20 minutes)

The Big Idea: Bad things happen when Christians behave like pagans.

Read 1 Corinthians 4:14–6:20 together. (This might seem like a lot of Scripture to read in one chunk, but the passage isn't actually all that long.)

> You'll need—
> • Bibles

Q: What seems to be the overall problem in this passage?

• What behavior does Paul describe that reveals that problem?

Q: What's your reaction to chapter 5, verses 9-12?

• How is this similar or different from what you've heard Christian leaders say about sexuality?

Explain: **Corinth was a place where the idea of sexual boundaries was unheard of. Well, that's not quite true. As most anywhere else, a minority of people thought sex was wrong no matter what and even looked down on sexual expression in the context of marriage. And, as most anywhere else, most people thought those people were crazy. In Corinth sex was everywhere for the taking, 24 hours a day, however you wanted it.**

> FYI: If you work with young students, you may want to highlight and focus on a few sentences in this extended text: 1 Corinthians 4:14-15; 4:18; 5:1-2; 5:9-13; 6:7-11; 6:18-20—with patience, older students can probably mine the passage for themselves.

Q: Look at chapter 6, verses 7-11. What stands out for you in that paragraph?

• Do you see a path weaving through Paul's argument? Or do you think he's all over the map here?

• When he concludes his list of wrongdoers with the words, "And that is what some of you were. But you were washed, you were sanctified, you were justified in the name of the Lord Jesus Christ..." (v. 11), what do you think he's saying about God's work in people's lives?

Continue reading at chapter 6, verses 12-13.

Explain: **Paul deflects the claim that Christians—of all people—should be able to do as they please because Christians—of all people—believe they are held fast by the mercy of God. It's an argument he deals with in detail in the fifth and sixth chapters of Romans. Here, he simply dismisses it on practical grounds:** *I have the right to do anything,* **you say—but we all know that some things are just not beneficial (and some things can turn around and bite you!).**

Q: Can you think of some behaviors (sexual and otherwise) that although they may be forgivable are still practically worthless—and may even threaten to become life-controlling habits?

Q: Have you ever thought that maybe you could get away with things you know are wrong because God loves you no matter what?

• How would you feel if someone who claimed to love you thought he could take advantage of you that way?

• Does it seem like a stretch to think God might feel betrayed, hurt, disappointed, maybe even angry about being treated with such disrespect?

Continue: **Paul brings it home in the final paragraph of chapter 6, from verse 18 to the end. Let's read it together.**

Q: If someone read this paragraph and asked, "What is Paul trying to get them to do?" how would you answer the question?

• If someone asked, "Why does Paul want that?" what would you say?

• What do you think it costs to truly honor God with our bodies?

• Do you think it's worth it? Talk about that.

Transition: **Let's see what we can do to put all this in the context of life in the world as we know it.**

HOW | What Difference Does It Make? (15 minutes)

The Big Idea: Testing convictions about sexual boundaries

Explain: **It's interesting how many people make significant decisions about sexual behavior because they don't think (or have forgotten how much) those choices matter.**

You'll need—
- Copies of the *What Difference Does It Make?* handout (on DVD) or Student Journal (**page 94**)
- 3 x 5 cards
- Pencils
- In advance ask six leaders or mature students to read the brief scenarios below as if the story were their own. The more they sell it, the better.

Distribute the *What Difference Does It Make?* handout and ask the first reader to step forward.

Encourage the group to give their best, most solid, biblical advice to each reader after he or she finishes.

Move the conversation along at a pace that makes sense in your group.

When you reach the end of the scenarios, take it to the next step.

Explain: **Lots of times there are special circumstances that might make it seem like it's more okay to cross boundaries that otherwise would be taboo. How would you respond to the following quick scenarios?**

- He's going to war and may not come home alive. May I?
- She has cancer—we don't know if they caught it in time. May I?
- We're going to be married in less than a year. May I?
- We're going to be married in less than a week. May I?

Explain: **Sometimes it's just so hard to say no. It's a bit like living in first-century Corinth where sexual involvement was pretty much assumed. How does someone follow Jesus under those circumstances?**

Q: What are some of the most convincing arguments that you should thoughtfully limit your sexual activity?

Q: Do you think fear is a good or a bad motivation for not engaging in sexual activity?

• How well have you seen that work out for people?

Q: What are some things we can do to talk sense to the raging hormones that nag us to seek sexual pleasure at any cost?

Q: How can we get support from other people—and give it, too—for where we draw our sexual boundaries?

• What sort of person would you feel safe going to when you struggle with proper sexual boundaries?

• Honestly, are you the sort of trustworthy person others can come to when they struggle with proper boundaries? Because...

At this point, distribute 3 x 5 cards to the students and ask them to write down three things:

    I. How far they choose to go sexually before they get married.

    II. The reasons they've chosen that point.

    III. Someone they'd be willing to talk with about their boundary decisions—someone who can and will hold them accountable (hopefully not just for the next week or two, but all the way until they hear "Here Comes the Bride" at their own wedding).

> FYI: In addition to religion, a number of other factors influence whether or not teenagers are virgins. Students are more likely to be virgins if they have...
> • A high level of strategic orientation
> • Educated parents
> • A low level of risk orientation
> • A high level of family satisfaction
> • A biologically intact family
> • Fewer dating relationships
> • Fewer friends having sex
>
> Mark Regnerus, *Forbidden Fruit* (New York: Oxford University Press, 2007), p. 126.

Recommend that each person keep his or her 3 x 5 card safe and bring it out every day for the next week as a reminder to pray for strength for everyone in the group.

Conclude by inviting several people to pray out loud as you close the session.

Other Resources for Teaching on Boundaries

NOW | Dirty Pictures (15 minutes)

The Big Idea: Pornography and lust go hand in...never mind.

Distribute the *Dirty Pictures* handout.

Explain: **Here's the origin of the word *pornography*:**

ORIGIN mid-19th century: from Greek *pornographos* "writing about prostitutes," from *porne* "prostitute" + *graphein* "write."

Q: What has *pornography* come to mean in your culture?

Explain: **There are lots of arguments about pornography:**
- **First Amendment arguments about protected speech**
- **Arguments about art and culture enlightenment**
- **Arguments about the amount of money pornography generates and who gets those dollars**
- **Arguments about human rights abuse and the objectification of women**
- **Arguments about the victimization and exploitation of children**
- **Arguments about community standards and perceptions**

Ultimately—although people don't always speak about it plainly—there's no argument about why people use pornography. A Kinsey Institute survey found the top five reasons people say they use porn:[24]

> You'll need—
> - Copies of *Dirty Pictures* handout (on DVD) or Student Journal (**page 96**).
> - Pencils

> FYI: It's difficult to talk about pornography in this context without moralizing. The issue is—at least from where we sit—so cut and dried that we may be putting you in a position to come across as just preachy. So we urge you not to talk too much. Let your group fill the silence when they're ready. Follow the admonition in James 1:19—"be quick to listen, slow to speak, and slow to become angry."

---

24. Michael Kirk and Peter J. Boyer, "American Porn," *FRONTLINE* (aired February 7, 2002), http://www.pbs.org/wgbh/pages/frontline/shows/porn/ (accessed July 15, 2008).

- **Number Five: To distract myself (38%)**
- **Number Four: Because I can fantasize about things I wouldn't necessarily want in real life (43%)**
- **Number Three: Curiosity (54%)**
- **Number Two: To sexually arouse myself and/or others (69%)**

All leading to...

- **The Number One Reason People Use Porn: To masturbate or for physical release (72%)**

Continue: **If fueling lust is *the point* of viewing, reading, and hearing pornography...I'm not sure I have an intelligent question to ask...I might as well ask if you think there's any upside to strangling kittens.**

PBS *Frontline* producers' interviews with porn industry insiders indicate that actresses in adult films have a career length of roughly one year.

Michael Kirk and Peter J. Boyer, "American Porn," *FRONTLINE* (aired February 7, 2002), http://www.pbs.org/wgbh/pages/frontline/shows/porn/business/ (accessed July 29, 2008).

Q: So, let me just ask you to talk about whether you're in any way surprised by that survey, or if it's about what you'd expect.

Explain: **Here's another finding from the Kinsey survey.**

Among those who use porn...[25]
- **80% say they're fine with their porn use.**
- **30% say they feel bad while using porn.**
- **19% say they're fine with it, but their partner doesn't (or wouldn't) like them using porn.**
- **16% say they feel bad after using porn.**
- **9% say they've tried to stop using porn but can't.**

Q: What's your reaction to those numbers?

Q: Can you think of anything we can do as a group to help the 9% of porn users who've tried to quit but can't?

---

25. Michael Kirk and Peter J. Boyer, "American Porn," *FRONTLINE* (aired February 7, 2002), http://www.pbs.org/wgbh/pages/frontline/shows/porn/ (accessed July 29, 2008).

• How about helping the 16% who feel bad after using porn or the 30% who feel bad *while* using porn?

• How about the people who love the 19% who believe their loved ones don't like them using porn (or wouldn't like it if they knew)?

Q: If you found out that your boyfriend or girlfriend was using porn, how would you feel? What would you say?

• If you found out that a friend was using porn, how would you feel? What would you say?

• If you found out that an adult you respected was using porn, how would you feel? What would you say? What would that do to your level of respect for this person?

Conclude this learning element with a final question:

Q: Going back up to the first set of findings, if a friend told you she was *curious* about pornography (like the 54% who say "curiosity" is their motivation for using pornography), what would you say to her, and why?

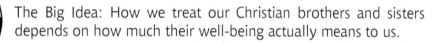

NOW | What Is Sexy? (10 minutes)

The Big Idea: How we treat our Christian brothers and sisters depends on how much their well-being actually means to us.

Explain: **We're going to make two lists of what's sexy—one for females and one for males.**

Proceed: **Girls, list all the things you think are sexy in boys. Boys, listen respectfully—and take notes.**

Continue: **Boys, list all the things you think are sexy in girls. Girls, listen respectfully—and text your friends.**

After both lists are complete, ask:

Q: Is there anything that surprises you about the other gender's list?

Q: Is there anything that makes you uncomfortable about the other gender's list?

Q: Do you think it's okay to be intentionally sexy if you have no intention of having sex? Discuss that.

Q: What are the potential benefits and risks of recognizing what is sexy?

Q: Suppose someone is tempted to mishandle the information we've shared about what is sexy. How might they mishandle it?

• How can we be accountable to each other for handling this conversation responsibly?

Distribute the *What Is Sexy?* handout.

You'll need—
• List-making supplies
• Copies of the *What Is Sexy?* handout (on DVD) or Student Journal (**page 98**)
• Pencils

FYI: This discussion is probably not suitable for young adolescents. Exercise discretion.

To keep things on track, separate the girls from the guys for simultaneous discussions; then come back together to share your results.

OR

Before the group discussion, ask the boys to listen silently while the girls make their list; then ask the girls to listen silently while the boys make their list.

Conclude by explaining: **Here are some additional questions for you to think about.**

As always, you can get in touch with me if there's anything you'd like to talk about before we're all back together.

NOW | Hooking Up, Oral Sex, Friends with Benefits (15 minutes)

The Big Idea: Hooking up, oral sex, and friends with benefits are not as widespread as reported.

Q: What do you think "hooking up" is all about? What do you think drives that?

• How about "friends with benefits"? What do you think drives that?

• How big a part do you think oral sex plays in hooking up and friends with benefits?

You'll need—
• Copies of the *Hooking Up* handout (on DVD) or Student Journal (**page 99**)
• Pencils
• Bibles

Distribute the *Hooking Up* handout and work through it together.

Here are some resources you can introduce to the conversation, if you wish.

FYI: A survey reported by NBC News and *People* magazine in January 2005 found that:[26]
• 8% of 13-to-16-year-olds (3% of 13-to-14- and 12% of 15-to-16-year-olds) said they'd been in casual sexual relationships with someone they were NOT (the questionnaire capitalized the word *not*) serious about and with whom they were not in love.

• Of those who said they'd had oral sex (12% of 13-to-16-year-olds),
- 78% said they'd had oral sex in a casual relationship
- 79% said they'd had sexual intercourse in a casual relationship
- Just 4% said they'd ever attended one of the widely reported but largely unsubstantiated oral-sex parties

FYI: In the January 2005 NBC/*People* magazine report on 13-to-16-year-olds, 12% of 13-to-16-year-olds (4% of 13-to-14- and 19% of 15-to-16-year-olds) said they'd had oral sex.

26. This NBC News/*People* magazine: National Survey of Young Teens Sexual Attitudes and Behaviors was conducted by Princeton Survey Research Associates International and cited by the Centers for Disease Control and Prevention in Sexual Behavior and Selected Health Measures: Men And Women 15–44 Years of Age, Advance data from vital and health statistics, 2005. http://www.msnbc.msn.com/id/6839072/%20(2%20of%208)2/2/08%205:15%20PM

A CDC report that same year—using data gathered in 2002—showed a sharply higher prevalence of oral sex among 15- and 16-year-olds (with 35% and 42% of boys and 26% and 42% of girls saying they'd had oral sex). Why the difference in the numbers?

- One possibility is that the CDC data—which were advance numbers—might be adjusted down in the final analysis.
- Another possibility is a flaw in the NBC/*People* data (none has been noted at this writing).
- A third possibility is something called *the cohort effect*, which reflects distinctive behaviors in a given age cohort that's only noticeable if the group continues to buck trends as they grow older.

Is it possible that oral sex peaked after 2002 and was declining by fall 2004 when the NBC/*People* surveys were conducted? Is it possible there was a dip in the numbers in 2004 that has since risen to 2002 rates or beyond? You work with kids; you know that attitudinal and behavioral differences exist from one graduating class to the next. Many things are possible.

Here's an idea: If you treat these reports like high-resolution photographs that record pretty accurately what was going on at the time they were taken, you'll be on safe ground. And you can invite your group to reflect on what they want the photograph that will characterize their sexual attitudes and choices to look like.

When you finish working through the handout…

Conclude with this: **Look at Colossians 3:1-14 and let's see if there's help in a passage that uses similar imagery.**

I'd like you to join me in praying out loud through this passage. Start at the first verse where someone might thank God that we've been raised with Christ. Then someone else might ask God to help her set her heart on things above—and so on. I'll close this time in a few minutes.

NEW | Dude, Your Sister's Hot! (20 minutes)

The Big Idea: Sex makes people do crazy things.

Read Genesis 26:1-14.

Q: What do you think of Isaac's strategy to save his own life?

You'll need—
• Bibles

• How do you imagine Rebekah felt about it?

• Would you have gone along if you'd been in Rebekah's sandals?

Look at Genesis 12:10-20 and 20:1-18.

Explain: **Does the phrase, "Like father, like son" mean anything to you? Can't you just imagine Isaac as a boy, sitting around the fire and listening to his dad, Abraham, tell this story?**

Look again at Genesis 26:8-9.

Q: What do you think tipped off the king that Isaac and Rebekah weren't brother and sister?

Explain: **The Hebrew word translated *caressing* in the TNIV suggests that Rebekah and Isaac were giggling and fooling around. When the king looked out his window, he could tell that, whatever they were giggling about, it wasn't a joke shared by healthy brothers and sisters.**

FYI: There are several similarities between Abraham and Isaac:
• Both are reported to have stayed in Gerar.
• Each asked his wife to pretend to be his sister.
• Both were rebuked by the king for the shame they could have brought to his people.

Q: How do you explain Isaac's choice to expose Rebekah to the risk of abuse?

• Do you think Isaac's fear was realistic?

Explain: **It's a good thing the king turned out to be a stand-up guy. And maybe it's worth noting that this is one of those times when the person who** claimed to follow God (Isaac) comes out looking somewhat worse than the pagan guy who is horrified that any of his people could have unknowingly slept with a married woman. Yet another reason why people like Isaac—and the rest of us—need God's mercy.

Conclude by inviting your group to pray together about trusting God to break you out of fear and unhealthy sexual patterns.

NEW | Being Careful **(30 minutes)**

The Big Idea: Being *careful* isn't as easy as it sounds.

Distribute the *Being Careful* handout.

Explain: **A few months after prom, Jimmy described what it was like to have sex for the first time. Here's what he said:**

Read (or have someone read) what Jimmy said from the handout, then walk through the questions together.

Saints Are Made, Not Born...

Explain: **Augustine was an important figure in Christian faith and theology in the fourth and fifth centuries. In his autobiography, *Confessions*,** Augustine admits a lengthy (and double-minded) struggle with lust.

> You'll need—
> • Copies of the *Being Careful* and *Saints Are Made, Not Born* handouts (on DVD) or Student Journal (**pages 102 and 106**)
> • 3 x 5 cards
> • Pencils

Look at the passage from *Confessions* on the *Saints Are Made, Not Born* handout, then answer the questions that follow.

Conclude this element by inviting your group to pray for the capacity to love each other and look out for each other, instead of thinking about how to gratify your own self-absorbed desires.

How | Why Wait? (15 minutes)

The Big Idea: Each of us is responsible for deciding whether or not to postpone sexual involvement until marriage.

Distribute the *Why Wait?* handout and give your group a few minutes to think and write.

You'll need—
• List-making supplies
• Copies of the *Why Wait?* handout (on DVD) or Student Journal (**page 108**)
• Pencils

The appeal of abstinence pledges diminishes as teenagers get older. In one national survey, just under 20% of 12-year-olds had pledged abstinence compared with 9% of 18-year-olds. For evangelical teens, 33% of 12-year-olds had taken an abstinence pledge compared with 16% of 18-year-olds.

Mark Regnerus, *Forbidden Fruit* (New York: Oxford University Press, 2007), p. 92.

Explain: **Let's create two lists from the point of view of ordinary students in ordinary public schools.**

• List One: What are some reasons that ordinary students in ordinary public schools give for having sex when people believe they're ready?

Q: What reasons do you find completely unconvincing? Why?

Q: What reasons would you have trouble arguing against? Why?

Q: Are there any reasons you're surprised you haven't heard people give?

• List Two: What are some reasons that ordinary students in ordinary public schools give for delaying sex until marriage?

Q: What reasons do you find completely unconvincing? Why?

Q: What reasons would you have trouble arguing against? Why?

Q: Are there any reasons you would add to the list? Why?

Q: Compared to this time last year, do you find yourself more or less sure of your convictions about sexual behavior—or about the same?

- More sure because...
- About the same because...
- Less sure because...

Q: Have your current convictions been tested?

- How did you resolve that challenge?

Q: What do you think it would take, if anything, to change your convictions?

Explain: **Ecclesiastes 4:12 reads:**
> Though one may be overpowered,
> two can defend themselves.
> A cord of three strands is not quickly
> broken.

Q: How do you think that idea applies to living true to our convictions about sexual behavior?

- Who else knows the strength of your convictions about this?

- How can you ask that person (or those people) to help you be true to what you believe is right?

Conclude by asking the group to stand in a circle and reach behind the ones immediately to their left and right and take the hand of the person standing one over in each direction so their arms are woven together. Invite them to pray for strength to respect the appropriate boundaries of their sexual behavior.

Teenagers who take a virginity pledge delay sexual intercourse and have fewer sexual partners than those who do not. However, the delay of first sexual intercourse is 21 months, with the average age being 18.8 for pledgers and 16.11 for non-pledgers. Approximately 75% of teens who make a promise to God, family, friends, future mate, and future children do not succeed in keeping that promise.[a] In addition, students who take a pledge are less likely to use a condom at first intercourse and are more likely to contract a sexually transmitted infection.[b] Furthermore, pledging adolescents were found to engage in other sexual behaviors (in other words, oral sex, anal sex) at greater rates than non-pledging adolescents.[c]

a. R. Rector, K.A. Johnson, and J.A. Marshall, "Teens Who Make Virginity Pledges Have Substantially Improved Life Outcomes," A Report of the Heritage Center for Data Analysis, Washington, DC: The Heritage Foundation (2004).

b. H. Brukner and P. Bearman, "After the Promise: The STD Consequences of Adolescent Virginity Pledges." Journal of Adolescent Health, 36 (2005): 271–287.

c. E.S. Lefkowitz, M.M. Gillen, C.L. Shearer, and T.L. Boone, "Religiosity, Sexual Behaviors, and Sexual Attitudes During Emerging Adulthood," The Journal of Sex Research, 41 (2004): 150–159.

HOW I 10 Ways to Say No (15 minutes)

The Big Idea: How to say NO even if a little part of you wants to say YES.

Q: How many ways can you think of to turn down someone who wants to take you farther sexually than you want to go sexually? Let's make a list.

Q: Do you think it's equally difficult for every person to hit the brakes sexually? Why or why not?

• Do you think there are some situations that make hitting the brakes more difficult? Why do you think that's so?

You'll need
• List-making supplies
• Copies of the *10 Ways to Say No* handout (on DVD) or Student Journal (**page 111**)
• Pencils

Q: Do you think there's a progression of sexual contact that's assumed by most people when they're going out? In other words, is there a set order in the way a relationship is assumed to develop sexually? If so, what does that look like?

If the group believes there is an assumed progression, write it where everyone can see. Then ask:

Q: How soon in a relationship do you think most people would expect to have each of those sexual experiences?

• What makes you think your perceptions about this are reality-based?

• Where do you think these sexual expectations come from?

• Do you think one gender drives these expectations more than the other? Why?

• How do you feel about that?

Q: If you were to view others as brothers or sisters in Christ, would that affect how you treat them sexually?

Conclude by distributing the *10 Ways to Say No* handout and inviting the group to reflect at a more personal level.

HOW | SexTalk: Boundaries (20 minutes)

The Big Idea: Finally, an answer to the question: "How far can I go?"

Play the DVD, then ask—

Q: What idea or phrase stuck with you from that piece?

Q: Why do you think that's significant?

Distribute the *SexTalk: Boundaries* handout.

Explain: **Lust is a serious fixation on something that's not mine to have; it's a deep, focused, inappropriate craving. In the biblical languages, the images associated with lust are heavy breathing, smoldering, and bursting into flames. The Bible doesn't talk about hooking up or friends with benefits; it talks about breaking boundaries to get what isn't mine to take.**

Q: What kind of damage have you seen lust do to people and relationships?

Q: Remember the line: "The trick is, not everybody lusts over the same things"? Does that ring true to you?

> You'll need—
> • A television or video projection unit
> • DVD player
> • The *Good Sex* DVD, cued to "SexTalk: Boundaries"
> • Bibles
> • Copies of the *SexTalk: Boundaries* handout (on DVD) or Student Journal (**page 114**)
> • 3 x 5 cards
> • Pencils
>
> If you have a talented actor or reader in your group, he or she could read "SexTalk: Boundaries" instead of you playing the DVD. The video transcript is on the DVD.

• So when he asks, "Why not ask each other—maybe anonymously—about what triggers lust?" what do you think about us doing that as a group?

Distribute 3 x 5 cards and pencils.

Explain: **I'd like for you to write things that typically tempt you to lust. I'm the only one who will see your cards, but I do plan to read them out loud without identifying who wrote them—which I probably won't even know because I'm going to shuffle the cards together as you bring them to me.**

Please be honest. I'll give you a couple of minutes to write and bring me your card.

Read the cards one at a time, filtering any that are spoofs. Take care not to register shock or disgust and don't belittle anyone's expression.

> FYI: Timothy was likely in his early 30s when Paul wrote this letter to him.

Q: What do you think we can do to help each other out with these temptations to lust?

• What can each of us do to take responsibility to avoid what tempts us?

Read 2 Timothy 2:22 together.

Q: What does this suggest about our responsibility?

• Compare that with James 4:7-10.

Q: What does this suggest about our responsibility?

> FYI: In this passage, James issues a series of 10 commands, the verbs of which call for an immediate response. James isn't shy; he's calling for immediate action.

Conclude: **Pray silently about the temptations you believe you need to flee—at least for the time being.**

Now pray silently about the temptations you believe you need to resist—at least for now.

Let's finish with prayers of hope that God will meet us where we are—and take us step by step to where we need to be.

HOW I Does Faith Matter? (10 minutes)

The Big Idea: Spiritual engagement makes a difference in sexual choices.

Distribute the *Does Faith Matter?* handout.

Explain: **The National Survey of Youth and Religion found that sexual attitudes and choices were strongly affected by the depth and breadth of adolescents' religious engagement.**[27]

> You'll need—
> • Copies of the *Does Faith Matter?* handout (on DVD) or Student Journal (**page 116**)

Go through the handout together.

Conclude this learning element by asking: **What can this group do to encourage us all to live out our values in our sexual behavior?**

---

27. The National Survey of Youth and Religion was reported in Christian Smith and Melinda Lundquist Denton, *Soul Searching: The Religious and Spiritual Lives of American Teenagers* (New York: Oxford University Press, 2005), Table 36.

SESSION 6

SESSION SIX | RESPONSIBILITY

For Your Own Preparation

Like it or not, each of us is responsible for our own sexual behavior. Acting as if it were true—actually taking responsibility—is what this session is about.

Sexual responsibility is a bit like following the rules of the road. Every state has some version of the Basic Speed Law, which states that motorists may drive only as fast as is reasonable under prevailing conditions. That means drivers must slow down on wet or slippery pavement, regardless of the posted speed limit, and no matter what others do. "Everyone else was driving 65!" is interesting but not fascinating if you skid into another car on a slick highway. You still get the moving violation. If you're lucky, that's all you get.

"Everybody does it!" is no excuse for behavior that violates the basic speed law of sexuality. You're not responsible for "everybody"—whatever they may be up to—but you *are* responsible for your sexual choices.

It's not hard to understand sexual responsibility. Just ask yourself, *What are the prevailing conditions of my life? Given these conditions, what is responsible sexual behavior?*

"Yeah, but you don't understand my situation: I'm not a slut or anything, but...I don't know, maybe I'm just hornier than most people."

That's an interesting theory; but if someone gets hurt, you're responsible for your behavior.

"No, but you don't understand. My girlfriend is really hot. I can't control myself."

Sorry, but if you lose control, that means you're driving too fast for prevailing conditions.

"But seriously, I think about sex all the time. That *is* my prevailing condition. Why would God give me hormonal surges and then tell me not to fulfill them? That's just mean."

It's not mean; it's a measure of human responsibility. If we were just like the other animals, things would be different. We're not. Humans have the capacity to live above our basic instincts, to live sacrificially, to live heroically.

"Fine, I'm responsible. Tell me to whom and for what, and I'll give it a shot."

Fair enough.

• We're responsible to God because God made us, and we belong to God before we belong to ourselves or anyone else.

• We're responsible to each other because we are brothers and sisters before we are anything else on the earth.

• We're responsible to ourselves because, even if we don't understand it, that inexpressible longing we feel is the longing to become what God made us to become.

The apostle Paul speaks:
> It is God's will that you should be sanctified: that you should avoid sexual immorality; that each of you should learn to control your own body in a way that is holy and honorable, not in passionate lust like the pagans, who do not know God; and that in this matter no one should wrong or take advantage of a brother or sister. The Lord will punish all those who commit such sins, as we told you and warned you before. For God did not call us to be impure, but to live a holy life.
> — 1 Thessalonians 4:3-7

In the first century, moral standards were generally pretty loose, and chastity was regarded as an unreasonable and unattainable standard. Paul, however, would not compromise. His definition of *sanctification* here is avoiding sexual immorality and learning to control our bodies in a way that's holy and honorable. But Paul also includes another component in his definition, one that smacks of responsibility: doing no harm to our sisters and brothers. You may not have to look any further than your own youth group to see out-of-control people taking advantage of their brothers or sisters in Christ. Pity.

If students are going to win the fight for holiness, their only hope is to ask Jesus to help them win it. That takes a more thorough conversion than many have yet experienced.

But then they also need to ask others to help them. Along with a deepening intimacy with the God who alone can sanctify and make us holy, acting responsibly takes support and accountability in the community of God's people.

Reflect for a Moment

We can't lead students where we're not willing to go ourselves. We can point them... but they'd rather be guided. Here are a few questions to consider as you prepare to lead this session on responsibility.

Q: What are some of your most rewarding experiences of sexual responsibility?

• Describe the cost of taking sexual responsibility.

Q: What are some of your most significant failures to take sexual responsibility?

• How do you think that happened?

• What did you learn about sex? About yourself? About others? About God?

Q: If you had just one hour to talk with kids about sexual responsibility, what would you try to communicate?

• Why do you think that's so important?

• If you were prevented from lecturing on the subject, how would you try to communicate during that hour?

NOW | SexTalk: Responsibility (15 minutes)

The Big Idea: We're more responsible to and for others than we might think.

Open: **When it comes to your sexuality, to whom do you think you're responsible?**

Explain: **There's a video I'd like you to see before we continue our conversation.**

> You'll need—
> • A television or video projection unit
> • A DVD player
> • The *Good Sex* DVD, cued to "SexTalk: Responsibility"

Play the DVD, then ask—

Q: How, if at all, does the video give a different answer to the question of who we're responsible to when it comes to our sexuality?

Q: Let's think about how our decisions affect people we know, and sometimes even people we don't know. I'm going to read off one person or group of people at a time, and let's think together about how our sexual choices affect them. Try to be as specific as you can, please.

> • Ourselves
> • The person(s) with whom we're sexually involved
> • Our friends
> • Our mom or stepmom
> • Our dad or stepdad
> • Our siblings
> • Our school
> • Our church
> • Our youth group
> • Our adult youth leader(s)
> • Our God

> Instead of playing the DVD, with a little preparation, you can have a student perform "SexTalk: Responsibility" as a monologue. The video transcript is on the DVD.

Q: If someone asked you why you're responsible to God for your sexual choices, what would you say?

• How about if you were asked why you're responsible to others?

Wrap up this discussion and begin transitioning to the NEW step by explaining: **It's partly because we in this room are responsible to and for each other that I think it's so important for us to have honest discussions about how our choices affect each other.**

NEW | The King and I (25 minutes)

The Big Idea: We're responsible to God and to others for our sexual choices.

Q: In general, what does it mean to be "responsible"?

Q: What do you think it means to be sexually responsible?

Odds are good that students will think about sexual responsibility as being responsible for only themselves. That's a good starting point, but it doesn't begin to touch our boundaries of responsibility.

Explain: **Using the story of David, today we're going to focus on two levels of responsibility that we all share when it comes to our sexuality:**
• **God**
• **Others**

You'll need—
• Copies of the *The King and I* handout (on DVD) or Student Journal (**page 120**)
• Pencils
• Bibles
• In advance scan through 2 Samuel 11 and be prepared to give a two-minute recap of the action.

Recap: At this point give a recap of what happens with David, Bathsheba, and Uriah from 2 Samuel 11.

Read 2 Samuel 12:1-13 aloud.

OUR RESPONSIBILITY TO GOD

Q: Do you think it was right for David to be set up like this by Nathan? Why or why not?

Q: Try to put yourself in David's shoes for a moment. How would you feel if you were hearing that stuff said right out loud?

• Would you be angry with God for telling Nathan about your personal life?

Q: How would you feel if your youth leader/pastor/minister went toe-to-toe with you over a sin that God had told her about you?

Explain: **David was a man specifically chosen by God—even before he was born—to be a special servant of God. That kind of choosing carries some pretty serious weight. David couldn't just go around doing whatever he wanted. He had a responsibility to the One who'd chosen him and blessed him beyond measure.**

FYI: To David's credit, he confeses to Nathan that he'd broken God's law. He could have denied it or defended himself; but instead, David accepted full responsibility.

Q: In what ways do we have a responsibility to God for our actions in general?

Q: When it comes to sex specifically, what responsibility do we have to God?

Q: David suffered severe punishment for neglecting his responsibility to God. When we do the same thing, what happens to us?

OUR RESPONSIBILITY TO OTHERS

Read 2 Samuel 12:1-25.

Explain: **What I want us to do is go through 2 Samuel 12:1-25 and count all the people who were affected by David's actions.**

Here is the cast of characters who were affected by David's irresponsibility as I counted them in this passage:
- God (vv. 8-9)
- Uriah the Hittite who dies (v. 9)
- The wife of Uriah, Bathsheba (v. 10)
- All of David's wives (v. 11)
- Bathsheba and David's first son who dies (v. 14)

Once you include all the people of Israel (who lost faith in their king as a spiritual leader because of this act), you have an uncountable number of people affected by David's irresponsible behavior.

Q: Can you think of a time when the actions of one person affected a lot of people?

Q: We've spent some time looking at how the sexual choices we make often have negative consequences for others. Could the opposite also be true—that the choices we make often have positive consequences for others? Can you give an example of this?

Read the following account to your students as an example of the way our decisions affect others.

> A few years ago, a college student told me she was pregnant, and I was the only one who knew. As we talked, it became clear she thought she wanted an abortion, but she didn't want to face that alone. She was no longer in contact with the father of the child. I suppose she felt pretty isolated. Finally, she asked if I'd go with her to the clinic.
>
> I said no. I told her I felt like going to the clinic would be supporting her choice to abort her baby and tried to convince her to look for another way. When the conversation ended, I guess neither of us felt like we got what we wanted from the other.
>
> A few days later, her sister came to town. Since the baby's dad was out of the picture, and since I wouldn't go, this student went to the clinic with her sister, even though she still wasn't positive she wanted the abortion.
>
> I always thought she made the wrong choice, but I've never been certain I made the right one. Was I as convincing as I could have been about my church's willingness to help her through the pregnancy, maybe help her with an adoption—whatever it might take to stand by her? Would she have made a different decision?
>
> What if I'd offered to go with her? That would have given her more time to think. Would she have made a different decision?
>
> Who knows?
>
> I just know I never felt like I handled that very well. I'd wish for another chance on this one, but honestly, I'm not 100 percent sure what I'd do.
>
> I feel bad about that, too.
> —KP

Explain: **Imagine that right now a young woman we know is sitting in a coffeehouse, wondering what to do about being pregnant. Let's say we knew that she was coming to us with this problem one week from today.**

Q: What would you want to be prepared to say to her?

• Is there anything that would keep you from saying that? What?

Q: Does going to the abortion clinic with her show more responsibility, or irresponsibility, toward her?

• How about toward God?

Continue: **Back to the story of David. We've already seen that he didn't act responsibly toward others, but the flip side of the story is someone who acted very responsibly. The prophet Nathan really stepped up to the plate and bore the responsibility to confront the king. This must have been a scary thing to do—Nathan easily could have lost his life since David had already killed one man to cover up his wrongdoing.**

In fact, one of the often overlooked elements of this story is what Nathan did *after* he confronted David. In 2 Samuel 12:25, we see that when Bathsheba has another son (Solomon), Nathan is the one who announces his birth. Nathan proclaims that the name "Jedidiah" would be attached to this son, meaning that this son is "loved by the Lord." Once Nathan acted responsibly and confronted David about his sin in the whole Bathsheba/Uriah mess, Nathan didn't just split. He stuck around and was part of God's redemption for David.

Q: What does 2 Samuel 12:25 tell you about sexual responsibility?

Q: If you wanted to act as responsibly as Nathan in the story about the college woman who had the abortion, what would you do?

• What would make it hard to do that?

• Given those difficulties, what would motivate you to stay in the woman's life?

To help students personalize the story of David and Nathan, use the material from the *The King and I* handout as background for large or small group discussion, or as a tool for individual personal reflection.

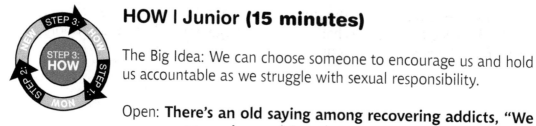

HOW | Junior (15 minutes)

The Big Idea: We can choose someone to encourage us and hold us accountable as we struggle with sexual responsibility.

Open: **There's an old saying among recovering addicts, "We are only as sick as our secrets." How does that saying relate to our responsibility to God and to others?**

Explain: **I want you to meet Junior.**

Play the DVD, then ask—

Q: What phrases or images in the video ring true?

Q: What's missing from the video, or what doesn't ring true?

Q: What do you think makes people hold onto their secrets and keeps them from sharing their struggles so others can help?

Q: Is this what keeps you from sharing your struggles?

Read the following quote from Dietrich Bonhoeffer to your students. He believed that this is the way Christians should think about each other—

> Yet even Paul said of himself that he was the foremost of sinners (1 Tim. 1:15)…There can be no genuine acknowledgment of sin that does not lead to this extremity. If my sinfulness appears to me to be in any way smaller or less detestable in comparison with the sins of others, I am still not recognizing my sinfulness at all. My sin is of necessity the worst, the most grievous, the most reprehensible…My sin is the worst…How can I possibly serve another person…if I seriously regard his sinfulness as worse than my own?[28]

Q: How big does Bonhoeffer think his sin is in comparison to others'?

You'll need—
- A television or video projection unit
- A DVD player
- The *Good Sex* DVD, cued to "Junior"
- Copies of the *Junior* handout (on DVD) or Student Journal (**page 122**)
- Pencils

Instead of playing the DVD, with a little preparation, you can have a student perform "Junior" as a monologue. The video transcript is on the DVD.

---

28. Dietrich Bonhoeffer, *Life Together* (New York: Harper and Row, 1954), pp. 96–97.

• What thoughts or feelings does that trigger in you?

Q: What responsibility do you think you have in sharing your sinfulness with God and with others?

Q: If you sense someone else is struggling with a sexual issue, what responsibility do you have to them?

• How might confession of your own sins play a part in your discussion about someone else's sins?

Q: What are some things you can do to become more responsible to God when it comes to your sexual questions and struggles?

Q: What are some things you can do to become more responsible toward others when it comes to your sexual questions and struggles?

(Note: If it feels appropriate, you can nudge students to think specifically about how they can be more responsible toward others in your youth group.)

Conclude by distributing pencils and copies of the *Junior* handout to each student. After giving them several minutes to complete it, have them huddle in groups with one or two other students to share one thing they've learned from this discussion and one way it will impact their sexuality.

Other Resources for Teaching on Responsibility

NOW | Getting Hitched (15 minutes)

The Big Idea: We can coach each other through any questions and struggles we have relating to dating or sex.

Open by explaining that you have a movie clip that explores how friends can help us navigate our sexual experiences and questions. Play the scene that starts when Hitch (played by Will Smith) says, "Now about the DJ...generally, I have a firm no-dancing policy." The clip ends at 52:05 when Will Smith says, "Get out," and slaps Albert Brennaman (played by Kevin James).

Play the DVD clip, then ask—

You'll need—
• A copy of the movie *Hitch* (Columbia Pictures, 2005), cued to 49:30
• A television or video projection unit
• A DVD player

Q: When has a friend tried to help you with some question or struggle you were having related to dating?

• What about that friend's help was actually helpful?

• What would have made it more helpful?

Q: Note that Albert ignores Hitch's advice. Why is it that we sometimes ignore our friends' advice?

Q: What kinds of things do teenagers talk about with their friends?

Q: One research study of teenagers showed that girls were more likely to be influenced by their friends' attitudes toward sex than boys were.[29] How does your own experience relate to that finding?

• If you think it's true that girls are more influenced by their friends' attitudes toward sex than boys are, why do you think that is?

---

29. Researchers at the University of Illinois at Chicago studied sexual attitudes and behaviors among 1,350 15-to-18-year-olds from across the United States. *Child Development*, Vol. 78, Issue 3 (May/June 2007), page 827, "Peer Selection and Socialization Effects on Adolescent Intercourse without a Condom and Attitudes about the Costs of Sex by Henry," DB, Schoeny, ME, Deptula, DP, and Slavick, JT (University of Illinois at Chicago)

• If you think that's not the case, can you explain your answer?

Q: What might keep guys from being influenced by their friends' attitudes toward sex?

• In what types of situations are guys the most open to the influence of their friends?

Q: What can we do to increase the level of trust and care we have for each other in this group?

• How big a part do the following elements play toward increasing trust?
—Honesty and openness
—Deep listening
—Willingness to learn from each other

Transition to the NEW step: **My hope is that for the rest of this discussion, as well as any discussion we have, we'll trust each other and care about each other enough to really listen and learn from each other.**

FYI: In 1985, Americans reported having three "core confidants" with whom they discuss important matters. In the 2004 General Social Survey, that number dropped to two. During the same time period, the percentage of Americans who named at least one non-kin person as part of this inner circle dropped from 80 percent to 57 percent.

Ann Hulbert, "The Confidant Crisis," The Way We Live Now, *New York Times*, July 16, 2006, http://www. nytimes.com/2006/07/16/ magazine/16wwln_lede.html?_ r=1&oref=slogin (accessed July 30, 2008).

NOW | Line Up (15 minutes)

The Big Idea: We might not always realize it, but we're influenced by the people around us.

Explain: **We're going to start with a little vision test.**

You'll need—
- Copies of the *Line Up* handout (on DVD) or Student Journal (**page 124**)
- Pencils
- A sheet of poster paper (or a whiteboard) on which you've drawn three lines of different lengths and labeled the three lines as "A," "B," and "C." Line B should be the longest, followed by Line A, with Line C as the shortest line.
- 10 volunteers
- In advance secretly ask eight students to raise their hands when you ask for volunteers to play Line Up. Explain that they should just play along and say that line A is the longest—no matter what anyone else says—and that there will be people who aren't in on the joke, so they shouldn't mention it when you send them out of the room.

Scale this to the size of your group: You can do the same thing with two or three set-up volunteers and one real volunteer per round. In fact, you can play just one round, if that fits better.

Ask for 10 volunteers (the eight you've secretly prepared in advance, plus two other real volunteers). Send four of your prepared volunteers and one real volunteer out of the room and out of earshot. (You may want to ask an adult to hang out with them, so they end up far enough away not to hear, but closer than the coffeehouse down the block.)

Explain: **I'm going to show you five volunteers three lines, and I want you to tell me which line is longest.**

Show the five remaining volunteers the three lines and "randomly" call on each of the five volunteers to pick the longest line. Of course, there's nothing random about it because you'll choose your four prepared volunteers first and your real volunteer last.

After the deed is done, explain to the audience and the one true volunteer that you prepared four volunteers ahead of time to see how the fifth person would respond.

Now the audience is in the know for round two and the next five volunteers. Repeat the process, choosing your four prepared volunteers first and your real volunteer last.

After the game is over, ask the two volunteers who weren't prepared in advance—

Q: How did you start to feel as you heard the others' answers?

• Why did you answer as you did?

• Was your confidence in yourself affected by the others' answers? Why?

Ask the audience:

Q: In the second round, once you knew what was going on, what did you notice?

• Think back to the first round—what did you observe then?

Q: What do you think you would have done if you were the real volunteer? Why?

Ask everyone:

Q: What does this say about the kind of influence we have on each other?

• Do you think our potential to influence each other creates any responsibility to look out for each other? If so, in what ways?

• Can you see this principle at work in the sexual influence we have on each other? Talk about that.

To help students personalize the issue of sexual influence and responsibility, use the *Line Up* handout as a tool for group discussion or personal reflection.

FYI: This learning exercise is based on an experiment devised by social psychologist Solomon Asch in 1951. In Asch's research, about seven percent of the subjects who were placed in this situation conformed to the clearly wrong majority at least once. Asch summarized, "The tendency to conformity in our society is so strong that reasonably intelligent and well-meaning young people are willing to call white black. This is a matter of concern. It raises questions about our ways of education and about the values that guide our conduct."

STEP 3:
STEP 1:
NOW
STEP 2:
NEW
HOW
STEP 1:
WON

NOW | This Is a Test (15 minutes)

The Big Idea: If you think you don't know someone with a sexually transmitted disease, think again...

Set up a continuum of 11 stripes of tape on the floor or 11 chairs or 11 sheets of paper on the wall. Label them from zero to 100 percent, like the following—

0%   10%   20%   30%   40%   50%   60%   70%   80%   90%   100%

Explain: **As I ask each question on this fact sheet, go stand beside the percentage marker that you believe is the closest to the correct answer.**

One at a time, read the statements on the *This Is a Test: Fact Sheet*. After getting your students to move to where they think the answer will be for each question, read the answer. Congratulate the students who got it right by throwing them some candy.

You'll need—
- A marker
- Candy
- Paper
- Masking tape
- 11 chairs
- A copy of *This Is a Test: Fact Sheet* (on DVD)
- Copies of the *This Is a Test* handout (on DVD) or Student Journal (**page 126**)
- Pencils

Ask your students to sit back down and discuss these questions:

Q: If a person knew he was infected, what obligation do you think he'd have to anyone he went out with? Why?

- What percentage of infected individuals do you think live up to those obligations? Why do you think that?

Q: Have you ever heard of anybody in your peer group going for a blood test to find out if she might be a carrier of an infectious disease?

- If not, why do you think you haven't heard of that?

- If so, how did that person feel about being tested?

- What were the results? And what did she do with the information?

- What advice would you want to give her?

Q: Given what you've just heard about the extent of sexual diseases, how likely do you think it is that you know someone who has one?

• If you have a suspicion that someone's sexual behavior might lead to a sexual disease, what's your responsibility to that person?

• If someone does, in fact, have a sexual disease, then what's your responsibility to that person?

To help students dive even deeper into the reality of sexually transmitted diseases and their responsibility, use the questions from *This Is a Test* handout for additional group discussion or personal reflection.

NEW | Roe v. Wade (25 minutes)

The Big Idea: Scripture can help us discern a responsible position on abortion.

Explain: **I'm going to read you some perspectives about abortion that you may have heard before today. If you agree with them, I'd like you to raise your hand. At times, I might see if any of you want to explain your opinions.**

You'll need—
• Bibles
• Copies of the *Roe v. Wade* handout (on DVD) or Student Journal (**page 128**)
• Pencils

• I don't believe (or think) it's ever okay to have an abortion. Raise your hand if you agree.

• I believe (or think) it's okay to have an abortion if the woman is raped. Do you agree?

• I believe (or think) it's okay to have an abortion if the health of the baby or the mother is in jeopardy.

• I believe (or think) the decision of whether or not to have an abortion is more the pregnant woman's decision than the baby's father's decision.

• I believe (or think) taking a "morning after" pill the day after you have sex is no different from aborting a baby two months later.

Q: What people, forces, or experiences have shaped your ideas about abortion?

• Have your ideas grown or changed over the years? In what ways?

Q: What's your understanding of God's attitude toward abortion?

• What's your understanding of God's attitude toward those who've had abortions?

• What's your understanding of God's attitude toward those who perform abortions?

• Can you support your understanding of these things with the Bible?

(Note: If your students need some help, you could try pointing them to Psalm 139:13-16, Exodus 23:7, Proverbs 6:16-17, and Jeremiah 22:3. On a related note, Job 3 and Jeremiah 20:14-18 give voice to the despair some people feel over this issue.)

Q: Why do you think people get so emotional about their views on abortion?

• How would you rate your emotional investment on abortion?

> FYI: As you read Proverbs 6:16-17, you might want to point out that Genesis 9:6 already prohibited the shedding of human blood because we're made in the image of God. As we can glean from Proverbs 6, shedding "innocent" blood may be an even more heinous crime against the image of God that lies within each of us.

Very
unsettled,
because...

Somewhat
unsettled,
because...

Completely
settled,
because...

Read the following arguments to your students.

For Abortion

• Legal abortions protect women's health.

• A fetus is not a child until it's born.

• Legal abortion supports a woman's right to choose.

Against Abortion

• Legal abortions threaten children's health.

• A fetus is an unborn child.

• Legal abortion destroys an unborn woman's right to choose.

- Compulsory pregnancy laws are incompatible with a free society.

- Access to safe abortions is the law of the land.

- People who are against abortion should also be against war and capital punishment.

- Abortion is birth control.

- Abortion is never wrong.

- Outlaw abortion, and more children will bear children.

- Sometimes abortion is the only option.

- Legalized abortion is incompatible with a free society.

- In this case, the law of the land is immoral.

- People who are against war and capital punishment should also be against abortion.

- Abortion is murder.

- Abortion is never right.

- Keep abortion legal, and more children will abort their children.

- There's always another option.

Q: Which of these arguments is most compelling to you? Why?

- Which is most aggravating? Why?

Q: Do you think our group has a responsibility regarding abortion? Talk about that.

To help your students personalize the controversial issue of abortion, use the questions from the *Roe v. Wade* handout for additional group discussion or for personal reflection.

NEW | The Home Front (25 minutes)

The Big Idea: Sexual responsibility also involves our parents.

Let the panel know it would probably be best if they left before you lead a discussion with the group, but offer to tell them about it later, if that's appropriate.

Open: Introduce the parent panel, explaining to your group that you've asked the parents to reflect on sexuality from their own point of view. Ask the parents on your panel these questions.

Q: Do you think it's different for teenagers today sexually than it was for you when you were young? Talk about that as personally as you can.

Q: What are your biggest fears about your kids' sexuality?

Q: How does your own sexual experience affect how you approach your kids' sexuality?

Q: Without naming names, what mistakes have you seen other parents make in handling their kids' sexuality?

> You'll need—
> • A few parent volunteers
> • Copies of *The Home Front* handout (on DVD) or Student Journal (**page 129**)
> • Bibles
> • Pencils
> • In advance invite a few parents to be part of a parent panel. Ideally, these parents would be people your students respect (which, by the way, doesn't mean they need to be "cool"). You might want to give them these questions ahead of time, so they can think about them and—if they wish—talk about their answers with their own kids before they come to the group.

Q: Without naming names, what wise choices have you seen other parents make in handling their kids' sexuality?

Q: Looking back, what do you wish you'd done differently in addressing your own kids' sexuality?

Q: In Exodus 20:12 and then later in Ephesians 6:1-4, children are commanded to honor their parents. How do you like to be honored by your kids in the middle of what they're experiencing romantically and sexually?

Q: What do you think a parent's responsibility is to his or her own kids when it comes to helping that kid understand his or her sexuality?

Give students a chance to ask their own questions. Then thank the panel and excuse them before debriefing the experience with your group by asking just the students the following questions:

Q: What's the most significant thing you heard from the parents panel?

• Why do you think that was significant?

• Did you hear anything that was confusing? Troubling? Angering? Surprising? Encouraging?

Q: Do you think sexual issues are different today than when your parents were young? Talk about that.

Q: Do you think parents should be concerned about what kids are going through sexually? Talk about that.

• Without naming names, what mistakes have you observed parents making in handling their kids' sexuality?

FYI: In Ephesians 6:4, Paul introduces a fresh element into family relationships by asking parents to consider their kids' feelings, which ran counter to the cultural assumption that the father's authority was absolute.

• Without embarrassing anyone, what mistakes have you observed kids making in responding to their parents' concerns about sexual issues?

• Is there anything you wish you'd done differently in communicating with your parents about dating or sex? Do you think you could revisit that now? Why?

Explain: **In Exodus 20:12 and Ephesians 6:1-4, we're given a word to describe what it means to act responsibly toward our parents: We're commanded to *honor* them.**

Q: What do you think is included in the idea of showing someone honor?

• How do you think you can honor your parents in the middle of what you're experiencing romantically and sexually?

• What do you wish your parents understood about supporting you as you grow to understand your sexuality?

• Why do you think teenagers don't talk to their parents about dating and sex? Or is that just a stereotype?

To help students consider what their own parents have contributed (and can still contribute) to their views of sex, use the questions from the *The Home Front* handout to guide additional group discussion or individual personal reflection.

HOW I Stopping Short (15 minutes)

The Big Idea: Our ability to act sexually responsible is often hindered because we stop short of asking the deeper questions and sharing our deeper experiences.

You'll need—
• Copies of the *Stopping Short* handout (on DVD) or Student Journal (**page 130**)
• Pencils

FYI: *Stepping* is a form of dance in which dancers' whole bodies are treated like percussion instruments, employing everything from handclaps to vocalization to stomps. Modern stepping is rooted in song and dance competitions popular in historically African-American fraternities and sororities for more than 150 years, with lots of embellishment along the way. Whatever you do, don't give the explanation we just gave you to your students. Instead, reference the 2007 movie *Stomp the Yard*, unless you know something better.

Read the following story to your students:
Here's what I wish I could take back…

I wish I could take back the silence. I wish I could take back my fear of asking the next question.

Demond and Chrissy had been dating for a while. Both were Christians, and both were friends of mine since we went to the same youth group. Chrissy also went to my school, and we were on the same step team, so I actually got to know her pretty well.

One day while Chrissy and I were riding home from step practice, she started talking about how much she was looking forward to going out with Demond that night. They hadn't seen each other in four days, and she was really missing him.

I asked, "So you and Demond are doing pretty well, huh?"

Chrissy paused a bit longer than I expected. "Yeah, I guess so."

She paused. (*I didn't imagine it; she definitely paused. Should I ask why? Or should I just let it go? I knew her well enough now. I decided to ask.*)

"What do you mean you guess so?"

Chrissy looked out the car window as if she were wondering how much to say. "We're doing more physically than I thought we would."

We pulled up to a stoplight. Neither one of us spoke. It was like we weren't sure where the conversation should go.

She'd apparently decided. "But it's okay. I really like him, and he really likes me. It's not like we're having sex or anything."

I sensed Chrissy wanted to switch subjects. I decided that was okay by me. I didn't know how to go any deeper, so I took the discussion toward the shallow end. "I'm sure you guys are fine." I paused for a second and then diverted the conversation. "I'm so tired of our step coach. It's like she thinks we don't have a life outside of step. I can't wait until summer."

Q: What did the narrator in the story do well?

• Can you identify anything she could have done to be more helpful to her friend? If so, why do you think she didn't take it to the next level?

(Note: feel free to read the story again, if that would help your students.)

Q: Why do we tend to "stop short" of asking each other questions that can help us all have more healthy relationships?

Q: What are some reasons we tend to "stop short" of volunteering information about what's going on in our sexual lives to friends who might be able to help us sort things out?

> Anything will give up its secrets if you love it enough. Not only have I found that when I talk to the little flower or to the little peanut they will give up their secrets, but I have found that when I silently commune with people they give up their secrets also—if you love them enough. — George Washington Carver

Q: How does either asking questions or sharing a personal story with someone express our responsibility toward that person?

• What do you think that costs?

• What do you think it's worth? Why?

To help students further realize how they can avoid stopping short in their relationships, use the questions from the *Stopping Short* handout for additional large or small group discussion, or possibly as a tool for individual personal reflection.

HOW | What Would You Do If... (15 minutes)

The Big Idea: Given all the sexual choices made by our friends today, we have countless opportunities to act responsibly.

Explain: **I'm going to read a number of quick scenarios. After each one, I want you to tell me what you'd do if this was happening to you.**

After each scenario, ask for volunteers to share what they'd do in response to the various situations. Try to draw out many different—and, if possible, contradictory—responses to these sticky situations. When students say they'd "talk to" their friend, ask them to specify what they'd actually say.

What Would You Do If...

• A guy on your football team is crushed that his prom date has to break their date because she's going to a family reunion. You find out from a friend at another school that she actually broke the date because she decided to go to that school's prom with another guy.

• You get two emails on the same day inviting you to the prom. You really want to go with Max, the guy who invited you second, but you feel like you should maybe accept the invitation from Ethan since it came first.

• You saw your cousin's girlfriend flirting with another guy at a party.

• A girl you liked was flirting with you for a while at a party, but then you find out that she actually came to the party with a different guy.

• You just found out that your best friend's boyfriend was cheating on her.

• You just found out that a girl in your math class, whom you barely know, has a boyfriend, and he's cheating on her.

• You just found out that Math Class Girl's boyfriend was cheating all right, but the person he was messing around with is one of your close friends.

• You hear from Kim that Lawana is being abused by her stepdad.

• Lawana tells you she's being abused by her stepdad.

After you've finished reading the scenarios, ask—

Q: Which situation was the easiest for you to decide how you should respond?

• What made it such a no-brainer?

Q: Which of these scenarios was the toughest for you?

• Why was it so hard?

Q: What thoughts went through your head as you were trying to decide how you should respond?

Q: What difference did the closeness of the relationship (e.g., your best friend versus a girl in your math class) make in your responses?

• What's good about that?

• What's not so good about that?

Q: What difference did your opinion of the severity of the behavior make in your responses?

• What's good about that?

• What's not so good about that?

FYI: According to data from the National Longitudinal Study of Adolescent Health, the greater the "density" of teenagers' friendship networks, the greater the influence of those friends. In a related finding, the study also indicates that the more religious a student's friends are, the less likely that student is to have sex.

Amy Adamczyk and Jacob Felson, "Friends' Religiosity and First Sex," *Social Science Research* 35 (2006): 924–947.

Distribute notepaper and pencils to your students and explain: **I'm guessing that at some point in today's discussion you've thought about someone you'd like to—or maybe you need to—act more sexually responsible toward. Maybe it's a friend who's headed down the wrong path, or maybe it's a student in your neighborhood who's making poor choices or who's the victim of other people's poor choices. On this notepaper, I'd like you to write a letter to that person describing your observations, as well as how you'd like to support and encourage him or her. You do NOT need to give this letter to that person. That's entirely up to you.**

After students have finished writing their notes, have them fold them up and hold the notes in their hands as you pray for God's grace to strengthen all of you to act responsibly toward those around you.

SESSION 7

SESSION SEVEN | DO-OVERS

For Your Own Preparation

Sooner or later, everyone needs do-overs.

But can we get them?

Children learn about do-overs in friendly games of hopscotch and marbles. A do-over is a second chance when someone makes a mistake; it's a gift between friends. No one has a right to demand do-overs; no one can say, "Shut up, I'm taking a do-over." A do-over is a favor; an act of grace.

Grace is what this chapter is mainly about—do-overs for people who commit sexual fouls. Which is to say, all of us.

First, some bad news: for single people, young and old, sex is a high-risk behavior, like driving under the influence. If nothing goes wrong, maybe nobody gets hurt; if things go badly, maybe someone dies.

That worst-case scenario—someone dies—raises the stakes from, say, *lying*. Tell a lie and, if things go badly, the worst that usually happens (for you, at least) is you get caught and suffer the consequences of breaking trust—unpleasant, but endurable.

Getting caught sexually includes outcomes like pregnancy and sexually transmitted infections.

Getting caught sexually may also include unanticipated emotional consequences. There's an interesting idea in Paul's first letter to the Christians at Corinth: "Flee from sexual immorality," he says. "All other sins people commit are outside their bodies, but those who sin sexually sin against their own bodies" (1 Corinthians 6:18). Sex has an unusually personal effect because it's uniquely *inside* rather than outside us; sex isn't something we merely *do*...

This makes sense to anyone who's been surprised to find herself feeling shame about something she's done. Some people respond to that feeling by building up calluses where the pain is—like the tough spots on a tennis player's hands or a dancer's feet. But, eventually, a lot of people decide it's just not worth it and shut down their sexuality.

Which is too bad. Good sex is very good—it's not the meaning of life, but it's a good thing. It's sad when a bad impression of a good thing follows people into adulthood.

All of which begs the question: Can 16-year-old boys and girls burned-out on premature sex get do-overs? Our answer depends on how we answer another question: Is God *for* us or *against* us?

If God is against us, it's Game Over; there won't be any do-overs. We'll die forgiven but still guilty. Don't say God didn't warn us.

If, on the other hand, God is for us, there's hope. We still must contend with the natural consequences of our behavior, but as Betsie ten Boom (who didn't survive the Nazi concentration camps) told her sister Corrie (who did): "[We] must tell people what we have learned here. We must tell them that there is no pit so deep that He is not deeper still."[30]

For people who grew up hearing about the irreversible effects of sexual failure—how much worse it is than other wrongdoing—this is hard to believe. But if the Bible is true, *this* is true: God's forgiveness covers every kind of wrong. Because God is gracious, people like us get a chance to begin again, starting right where we are (even though it's not where we're supposed to be).

Just to be certain we've said it, let's embrace one lonely group of people who need do-overs in spite of themselves. They are the ones who were (or, God forbid, *are*) abused by their fathers, brothers, sisters, uncles, aunts, cousins, babysitters, teachers, pastors, and boyfriends. (If we've left out anyone, it's only because we can't bear to go on.)

30. Corrie ten Boom and Elizabeth and John Sherrill, *The Hiding Place*, 35th anniv. ed. (Grand Rapids, MI: Chosen Books, 2006), p. 227.

These victims of sexualized violence tend to blame and punish themselves for what was done *to* them (not *by* them).

Hard as it may be to accept, this session points to the One who "heals the brokenhearted and binds up their wounds" (Psalm 147:3). If we do nothing else with do-overs, can we please offer sanctuary and hope to victims of sexual violence?

Reflect for a Moment

We can't lead students where we're not willing to go ourselves. We can point them... but they'd rather be guided. Here are a few questions to consider as you prepare to lead this session on do-overs.

Q: Write a few paragraphs (or pages, if you prefer) about your personal history with sexual do-overs.

• Who else knows your history?

Q: Is there anything in your sexual history that remains a closely guarded secret? Spend some time thinking, writing, or talking with someone about that.

Q: If you've been the victim or perpetrator of any form of sexual abuse, what did you do about that?

• To what degree do you consider that to be firmly in your past? What kind of unfinished business is there? What remains to be done?

Q: How did you reach your current understanding about do-overs?

Q: Think for a moment about the people in your group. Do you have reason to believe that any of them need sexual do-overs?

Q: If you had just one hour to talk with kids about sexual do-overs, what would you try to communicate?

• Why do you think that's so important?

• If you were prevented from lecturing on the subject, how would you try to communicate during that hour?

NOW | *Les Miserables* (15 minutes)

The Big Idea: Do-overs give fresh starts.

FYI: The choice between recommending NOW | *Les Miserables* and NOW | SexTalk: Do-Overs (**page 232**) was a toss-up for us. If you have time, take a peek at both before you decide.

Play the video, then ask—

Q: If you were the Bishop, what do you think you would have said when the police brought the thief back with the stolen silver?

Q: Obviously, the criminal didn't deserve the do-over the Bishop gave him. Why do you think the Bishop showed such remarkable grace?

• How do you think you would have felt if you were the man?

• What do you think the Bishop was feeling?

Q: What do you think the Bishop hoped the man would do with his life?

Q: Can you think of any other examples of incredible do-overs in books, movies, or real life? Briefly describe what happened and what the people involved did with their do-overs.

Q: Can you think of a time when you got a do-over you desperately needed? If so, can you tell that story?

Transition: **Let's see what the Bible says about do-overs.**

You'll need—
• A television or video projection unit
• A DVD player
• A copy of the movie *Les Miserables* (Columbia Pictures, 1998; starring Liam Neeson, Geoffrey Rush, Claire Danes, + Uma Thurman) cued to the clip approximately three minutes from the opening Columbia Pictures graphic, beginning with the line, "You can't sleep here." The clip ends about six minutes later with the Bishop's line, "And now I give you back to God."

FYI: In this scene, Jean Valjean (Jon Val-jon) (played by Liam Neeson) is on his way to report to his parole officer. He's told he can't sleep on the street, so he finds a meal and a bed at the home of a Bishop (played by Peter Vaughan). In the middle of the night, the ex-prisoner wakes and steals the Bishop's fine silver. He's later caught by the police. What happens next is a remarkable example of do-overs.

NEW | Clean or Unclean? (15 minutes)

The Big Idea: Exploring the tension between punishment and mercy for sexual wrongdoing

Read (or have someone read) Leviticus 20:9-22 in ominous tones.

You'll need—
- Bibles
- Copies of the *Clean or Unclean?* handout (on DVD) or Student Journal (**page 135**)
- Pencils

Q: This is an interesting list of no-nos. Do you think it's exhaustive—meaning, if something isn't on a list that goes into this kind of detail, do you suppose that means the omitted item is okay?

Q: How do you account for the harshness of the penalty for these acts? (I mean, "kill them" is not exactly the same as "get them into a 12-step group.")

Read John 8:1-11 together.

FYI: *Holiness* is purity. To be holy is to be all one thing, unadulterated by anything else. Procter & Gamble used to say of their flagship product, "Ivory Soap is 99 and 44/100ths percent pure," which is to say—not quite holy.

Q: How does this story compare to the commands in Leviticus 20?

- What's similar in the two passages?

- How are the two passages different?

Q: The woman appears to have been caught right in the act of adultery. Why do you suppose they brought the woman—but not the man—to Jesus?

I heard someone say once that perhaps Jesus was writing in the sand the names of all the women the Pharisees and teachers of the law had slept with in the past.
—KP

Q: If you were going strictly by the rules, is there any question this woman was guilty?

Q: Do you know what it feels like to be caught in the act of...whatever? Is someone willing to share a story about that with the rest of us? *(Note: This would be a really good time to make the room safe by going first.)*

Q: What do you think about what Jesus did here?

• What do you imagine he wrote in the dirt?

Explain: **John doesn't tell us what Jesus wrote, but whatever it was, it certainly shut down the party. Your Bible probably includes a note that this story isn't in the earliest and best manuscripts. William Barclay offers an opinion about why:**

> Augustine gives us a hint. He says that this story was removed from the text of the gospel because "some were of slight faith," and "to avoid scandal." We cannot tell for certain but it would seem that in the very early days the people who edited the text of the New Testament thought that this was a dangerous story, a justification for a light view of adultery, and they therefore omitted it. After all, the Christian church was a little island in a sea of paganism. Its members were so apt to relapse into a way of life where chastity was unknown, and were forever open to pagan infection. But as time went on, the danger grew less, or was less feared, and the story, which had always circulated by word of mouth and which one manuscript retained, came back....We may be sure that this is a real story about Jesus, although one so gracious that for a long time people were afraid to tell it.[31]

Q: With whom do you identify most in this story? The legal experts? The woman? Jesus?

Q: What conclusions do you draw from this story?

Q: Does it make sense to you that part of do-overs is the chance to get it right—or, in this case, stop getting it wrong? Talk about that.

FYI: One theory holds that the accusers had a special vendetta against the woman.

Another theory imagines the man was part of an elaborate trap. In verse five the accusers quote the law of Moses (sort of—Leviticus 20 calls for the man in this situation to be executed, too.)

Further complicating the matter, if Jesus said the woman should be executed, then he'd be inciting the people to break a Roman law prohibiting execution by local governments, and he'd lose his reputation as a friend of sinners (Luke 7:33-35). On the other hand, if Jesus said the woman should simply be set free, it would appear that Jesus was ignoring the Jewish law. If it was a trap, then it seems like a pretty good one.

FYI: As is so often the case, Paul points his readers to the example of Jesus in 1 John 3:3. Far from a legalistic obedience, Paul invites his readers—and us, for that matter—to follow Jesus' example of purity.

---

31. William Barclay, *The Gospel of John, Vol. 2* (Philadelphia: Westminster John Knox Press, 1975) pp. 291–292.

Q: Compare your thoughts about this with 1 John 3:1-10. What do you think John is getting at here?

Explain: **It's important to note that the broader context of 1 John makes it clear he's not talking about absolute and immediate perfection.**
- **He says in the first chapter that if we say we don't sin, we're only fooling ourselves.**
- **Then he says we should confess our sins and trust God to forgive us and cleanse us.**
- **In the second chapter, John says when we sin, Jesus takes our side and guarantees our forgiveness with his own life.**
- **Now in the third chapter—you'd have to be fluent in ancient Greek (or read a commentary) to catch this nuance—John says one mark of God's children is they don't *deliberately and consistently* go against what God wants.**

Continue: **Emo Philips had a joke about this kind of thinking: "When I was a kid, I used to pray every night for a new bike. Then I realised, the Lord doesn't work that way. So I just stole one and asked Him to forgive me...and I got it!"[32]**

To repent is to come to your senses. It is not so much something you do as something that happens. True repentance spends less time looking at the past and saying, "I'm sorry," than looking at the future and saying, "Wow!"
— Frederick Buechner, *Wishful Thinking*

Frederick Buechner, *Wishful Thinking: A Seeker's ABC* (New York: HarperCollins, 1973) p. 79.

Q: Do you see anything wrong with Emo's picture? Talk about that.

Q: What advice would you give someone who makes bad sexual choices over and over and seems to take do-overs for granted?

Q: How hard is it to just stop doing those things that have entrapped us in the past?

Distribute the *Clean or Unclean?* handout and work through the questions together.

When you reach the end of the handout...

---

32. Emo Philips, "The Best God Joke Ever—and It's Mine!" *The Guardian*, September 29, 2005, http://www.guardian.co.uk/g2/story/0,3604,1580452,00.html (accessed July 30, 2008).

Conclude by inviting your group to—
• Thank God for mercy.
• Ask God to help you not make the same mistakes over and over.

STEP 3:
HOW

STEP 3:
NEW
HOW
STEP 1:
STEP 2:
NOW

HOW | Who Me? (20 minutes)

The Big Idea: Common examples of folks who need do-overs and our own need for a fresh start

You'll need—
• Copies of the scenarios for selected readers
• Copies of the *Who Me?* handout (on DVD) or Student Journal (**page 136**)
• Pencils

FYI: A 2005 report found—
• One-third (33 percent) of sexually active teenagers ages 15 to 17 disclosed "being in a relationship where they felt things were moving too fast sexually," and 24 percent had "done something sexual they didn't really want to do."
• More than one in five (21 percent) reported having oral sex to "avoid having sexual intercourse" with a partner.
• More than a quarter (29 percent) of teenagers ages 15 to 17 reported feeling pressure to have sex.
• Nearly one in 10 (nine percent) of ninth through twelfth grade students reported having been physically forced to have sexual intercourse when they didn't want to. Females (12 percent) were more likely than males (6 percent) to report this experience.

Kaiser Family Foundation, "U.S. Teen Sexual Activity," January 2005, http://www.kff.org/youthhivstds/upload/U-S-Teen-Sexual-Activity-Fact-Sheet.pdf (accessed July 30, 2008).

Explain: **One of Hemingway's stories begins like this:**
Madrid is full of boys named Paco, which is the diminutive of the name Francisco, and there is a Madrid joke about a father who came to Madrid and inserted an advertisement in the personal columns of *El Liberal* which said: PACO MEET ME AT HOTEL MONTANA NOON TUESDAY ALL IS FORGIVEN PAPA and how a squadron of Guardia Civil had to be called out to disperse the eight hundred young men who answered the advertisement.[33]

Q: Hemingway's narrator describes the "all is forgiven" story as a joke. Does it sound funny to you? Talk about that.

• You don't have to tell it, but does anyone here have a story about wishing you could get a fresh start with someone important to you?

Distribute the *Who Me?* handout.

Explain: **Let's look at the first story on the handout. Follow along, then we'll talk about it.**

Read the Luke story, then ask—

---

33. Ernest Hemingway, "The Capital of the World," in *The Complete Short Stories of Ernest Hemingway*, The Finca Vigía ed. (New York: Simon & Schuster, 1987), p. 29.

Q: If you'd known each other, where along the way might you have said, "Luke, let's do something else right now?"

• On a scale of 1 (low) to 10 (high), how much help is that for Luke right now?

Q: Luke just came clean with this story. What do you want him to know first?

• What else do you want Luke to know?

• Anything else?

Explain: **Remember from the passage we just read that the religious leaders brought a woman caught in the act of adultery to Jesus. Suppose the one they brought was Luke, caught masturbating with a hardcore magazine in front of him. Jesus stoops down and starts writing in the dirt.**

When they kept on questioning Jesus, he straightened up and said to them, "Let any one of you who is without sin be the first to throw a stone at Luke." Again he stooped down and wrote on the ground. At this, those who heard began to go away one at a time, the older ones first, until only Jesus was left, with Luke still standing there. Jesus straightened up and asked him, "Luke, where are they? Has no one condemned you?"

"No one, sir," Luke said.

"Then neither do I condemn you," Jesus declared. "Go now and leave your life of sin."

Q: From the sound of Luke's account, how easy do you think it will be for him to hear these words of Jesus for himself?

Q: What do you think "Go now and leave your life of sin" means for Luke?

• If you were Luke's friend, what could you do to help him go and leave his life of sin?

Explain: **The second story on the handout is from Megan.**

Read the Megan story, then ask—

Q: Megan just told you this story. What do you want her to know first?

• What else do you want Megan to know?

• Anything else?

Q: Why do you think Megan feels dirty?

Q: Megan was the victim—is there any sense in which she may still need do-overs?

• If so, how would her do-over be different from the one her uncle needs?

The soldiers are there with their swords and lanterns. The high priest's slave is whimpering over his wounded ear. There can be no doubt in Jesus' mind what the kiss of Judas means, but it is Judas that he is blessing, and Judas that he is prepared to go out and die for now. Judas is only the first in a procession of betrayers two thousand years long. If Jesus were to exclude him from his love and forgiveness, to one degree or another he would have to exclude mankind.
— Frederick Buechner, *The Faces of Jesus*

Frederick Buechner, *The Faces of Jesus* (Harper & Row), p 148.

• If you don't think Megan needs a do-over, what *does* she need to get a fresh start after all this time?

C. S. Lewis wrote in *Reflections on the Psalms*:
There is no use in talking as if forgiveness were easy. We all know the old joke, "You've given up smoking once; I've given it up a dozen times." In the same way I could say of a certain man, "Have I forgiven him for what he did that day? I've forgiven him more times than I can count." For we find that the work of forgiveness has to be done over and over again.[34]

Q: How do you respond to that?

• How do you think Megan would respond?

Q: If you were Megan's friend what could you do to help her keep going forward?

Q: What do you imagine Jesus saying to Megan?

Explain: **Here's Taylor's story—it's on your handout.**

_____
34. C. S. Lewis, *Reflections on the Psalms*, (New York: Harcourt Brace Jovanovich, 1964), pp. 24–25.

Read Taylor's story, then ask—
Q: Taylor just told you this story. What do you want her to know first?

• What else do you want Taylor to know?

• Anything else?

Q: Taylor is angrier at herself than the boy who assaulted her. What's that about?

• She blames herself for what happened. Do you? Talk about that.

Q: You're the first person she's told; who else needs to know?

Continue: **Once again, picture Jesus as he stoops down and starts writing in the dirt. Taylor is standing there, watching him write as the accusations fly. Only now it's not other people accusing Taylor; it's Taylor accusing herself. How does she answer when Jesus asks, "Taylor, where are your accusers?"**

Carl Jung wrote in *Modern Man in Search of a Soul*:
> That I feed the hungry, that I forgive an insult, that I love my enemy in the name of Christ—all these are undoubtedly great virtues. What I do unto the least of my brethren, that I do unto Christ. But what if I should discover that the least amongst them all, the poorest of all the beggars, the most impudent of all the offenders, the very enemy himself—that these are within me, and that I myself stand in need of the alms of my own kindness—that I myself am the enemy who must be loved—what then?[35]

Q: What would you say to Taylor about forgiving herself?

• What would you say is the difference between truly forgiving yourself and simply letting yourself off the hook?

Q: I'm not asking you to tell it now, but I'd like to know how many of us have a story about finding a way to forgive ourselves that we might share with a person in Taylor's shoes.

For more on dealing with sexual abuse and other tough stuff, see **pages 259-261** in this guide and direct students to **pages 159-161** in the Student Journal.

35. C. J. Jung, *Modern Man in Search of a Soul* (New York: Harcourt, Brace and World Harvest Books, 1933), p. 235.

• Talk about the risk of sharing that kind of story.

• For those of us who have that kind of story, I'm curious to know how many of us have told it to help someone else.

Q: What's the most significant thing you're taking away from these stories?

• Why is that significant to you?

• What kind of help do you think you could use to follow through?

Conclude by asking people to get into groups of three or four of the same gender, making sure no one is left out.

Explain: **I don't know anyone who doesn't—or won't eventually—have a deeply felt need for do-overs. I look around this room, and I know that's true. I look in the mirror, and I *really* know it's true.**

I'd like you to do at least two of three things as we close:

> **1. If you know someone who needs do-overs, without disclosing who that is, briefly outline the situation and ask your circle what they'd do, if they were in your shoes, to help your friend—just to see if you can get any fresh ideas that might help you help your friend.**

> **2. If you know you need do-overs for something you haven't dealt with, say as much about that as you feel safe saying. Maybe that's just, "I need do-overs, but I'm afraid to talk about it right now." And maybe it's, "I need do-overs and here's why." Or maybe you're the "friend." However you feel most comfortable.**

> **3. Pray for each other. Pray for whatever it takes to trust the God of Do-Overs who loves us exactly as we are and loves us far too much to leave us that way.**

As you finish, if there are others still sharing stories and praying, I'll ask you to remain in your circle and visit quietly until I ask for everyone's attention at the end.

Two other things: First, I want to remind you of our agreement to keep things shared in this room appropriately confidential. Second, if you believe you're in over your head in any of this, please allow me to help you or get you to someone who can.

Other Resources for Teaching on Do-Overs

NOW | SexTalk: Do-Overs (15 minutes)

The Big Idea: One of life's biggest questions goes something like this: "I know I don't deserve it, but can I get do-overs?"

Play the video, then ask—

Q: What stands out for you in that video? Why do you think that's significant?

You'll need—
- A television or video projection unit
- A DVD player
- The *Good Sex* DVD, cued to "SexTalk: Do-Overs"

Instead of playing the DVD, with a little preparation, you can have a student perform "SexTalk: Do-Overs." The video transcript is on the DVD.

Q: Without giving away identities, describe someone you know who needs sexual do-overs.

- How much have you been able to help this person?

Q: Again, without giving away identities, describe someone you know who's really getting sexual do-overs and seems to be bouncing back.

Explain: **The closing lines from the video are: *Here's to the God who knows exactly what it costs to cancel our debts—the God who knows, firsthand, what it takes to heal our broken hearts. Here's to the Father of compassion and the God of all comfort—here's to the God of do-overs.***

Now listen to Colossians 2:13-15:

When you were dead in your sins and in the uncircumcision of your sinful nature, God made you alive with Christ. He forgave us all our sins, having canceled the charge of our legal indebtedness, which stood against us and condemned us; he has taken it away, nailing it to the cross. And having disarmed the powers and authorities, he made a public spectacle of them, triumphing over them by the cross.

Q: How do you think what Jesus did works to give us a shot at sexual do-overs?

Conclude this element by inviting the group to give thanks for God's guarantee of do-overs.

NEW | Scarlet Lady (20 minutes)

The Big Idea: The profile of a person who got serious do-overs from God

If your group is largish, break them into teams of half a dozen with the following assignment:

Explain: **I'd like each group to read Joshua 2:1-21, Joshua 6:20-25, Hebrews 11:31, and James 2:25. Then write a "Once upon a time…" story about Rahab, including what you take to be the moral of the story. When you're done, I'll ask you to read your story to the rest of us. You have 10 minutes.**

(Note: Do everything you can to ensure that each group receives wild applause for their efforts.)

> **You'll need—**
> • Bibles
> • Copies of the *Scarlet Lady* handout (on DVD) or Student Journal (**page 142**)
> • Paper
> • Pencils

> For variety, assign one or more groups to the same task with Hosea 1:1-9 and 3:1-5.

Q: What do you think is the most important thing that comes out of Rahab's story?

• Why do you think that's important?

Q: Why do you think God works with people like Rahab? Why not stick to virtuous Queen Esther or Joan of Arc types?

Read 1 Corinthians 1:26-31 together.

Q: What connections can you make between this and the story of Rahab?

To help students further personalize the story of Rahab and apply it to their own lives, use the questions from the *Scarlet Lady* handout in large and small group discussions, or as a tool for individual reflection.

> FYI: In 1 Corinthians 1:31, Paul is quoting from Jeremiah 9:24, which reads: "'Let those who boast boast about this: that they understand and know me, that I am the Lord who exercises kindness, justice and righteousness on earth, for in these I delight.'"

NEW | A Moveable Feast (15 minutes)

The Big Idea: Jesus embraces people who love him—no matter where they come from.

You'll need—
• Bibles
• Copies of the *A Moveable Feast* handout (on DVD) or Student Journal (**page 143**)
• Pencils

Consider getting someone to partner with you by reading the passages from Luke.

FYI: A *moveable feast* is a Christian celebration (like Palm Sunday) that moves relative to Easter, rather than being on a set date. Here, the term celebrates the good news that everybody's welcome at the table when Jesus shows up.

Explain: **I want you to put yourself in the scene we're about to read from Luke 7:36-50. Imagine yourself as someone waiting tables. You go into the kitchen, shaking your head. The cook says, "What? Is something wrong with the food?" "Nope," you say, "the food is great, but there's this woman out there..."**

This is Luke 7:36-38—
When one of the Pharisees invited Jesus to have dinner with him, he went to the Pharisee's house and reclined at the table. A woman in that town who lived a sinful life learned that Jesus was eating at the Pharisee's house, so she came there with an alabaster jar of perfume. As she stood behind him at his feet weeping, she began to wet his feet with her tears. Then she wiped them with her hair, kissed them and poured perfume on them.

Q: If you're waiting tables at this event, what do you imagine you'd be thinking about all of this?

Continue: **The cook goes into the dining room on the pretense of seeing that everything is okay. He comes back shaking his head. He says, "I don't know this Jesus character, but I sure recognize the hooker.* Isn't Jesus an evangelist or something? What's his story?"**

Suppose you've been watching the whole Jesus thing unfold. You work lunches and dinners, but you have some free time most mornings. So you've heard Jesus speak a couple of times; heard rumors about healing and whatnot; just heard him tell followers of John the Baptist, "Go back and report to John what you have seen and heard: The blind receive sight, the lame walk, those who have leprosy are cleansed, the deaf hear, the dead are raised, and the good news is proclaimed to the poor. Blessed is anyone who does not stumble on account of me" (Luke 7:21-23).

Now the cook, who is more or less your boss, is asking why Jesus would allow this particular woman, of all people, to make a spectacle of herself with him.

Q: What do you tell him?

Continue: **This is verse 39: "When the Pharisee who had invited him saw this, he said to himself, 'If this man were a prophet, he would know who is touching him and what kind of woman she is—that she is a sinner.'"**

Q: How long do you think Jesus would last on the staff of a modern church or Christian organization? Why?

Continue: **Simon, the religious leader hosting the dinner, "said to himself, 'If this man were a prophet, he would know who is touching him and what kind of woman she is.'" Simon mutters this under his breath; and Jesus responds.**

This is Luke 7:40-43.
> Jesus answered him, "Simon, I have something to tell you."
>
> "Tell me, teacher," he said.
>
> "Two people owed money to a certain moneylender. One owed him five hundred denarii, and the other fifty. [A denarius is about a day's wages for an ordinary working man. So the first guy owed about two years' wages if he didn't need to spend money on anything else—which, of course, he did. So it was the kind of debt that working people tend to never quite recover from, what with medical bills, rising fuel costs, and the like.] Neither of

* We don't know beyond a shadow and doubt that the unnamed woman in Luke 7:37 was a prostitute—only that Luke described the actions of "a woman in that town who had lived a sinful life..." William Barclay represents the woman as a notorious sinner in his commentary on Luke: "The woman was a bad woman, and a notoriously bad woman, a prostitute." John Gill's exposition on Luke also calls the woman "a notorious sinner...; a lewd woman, a vile prostitute, a harlot" and adds the original language "signifies both a sinner and a whore" (citing Castell. Lex. Heptaglott. col. 1195). Some have leapt to the conclusion that this story refers to Mary Magdalene, but that possibility seems unlikely since Mary is introduced by name later in Luke 8.

them had the money to pay him back, so he forgave the debts of both. Now which of them will love him more?"

Simon replied, "I suppose the one who had the bigger debt forgiven."

"You have judged correctly," Jesus said.

Continue: You're standing next to the cook when Jesus says this. He wipes a hand on his apron and looks at you like, "Well, that's a no-brainer."

Q: Is it a no-brainer? Do you think people who believe that God has forgiven a debt greater than they could pay seem to love God more than the ones who have a less-desperate picture of how much they owe God? What feeds your opinion about this?

Continue: Here's the big finish in verses 44-50:
Then he turned toward the woman and said to Simon, "Do you see this woman? I came into your house. You did not give me any water for my feet, but she wet my feet with her tears and wiped them with her hair. You did not give me a kiss, but this woman, from the time I entered, has not stopped kissing my feet. You did not put oil on my head, but she has poured perfume on my feet. Therefore, I tell you, her many sins have been forgiven—as her great love has shown. But whoever has been forgiven little loves little."

Then Jesus said to her, "Your sins are forgiven."

The other guests began to say among themselves, "Who is this who even forgives sins?"

Jesus said to the woman, "Your faith has saved you; go in peace."

Q: Do you think most Christians really believe Jesus when he says things like he said about (and to) this woman? Talk about that.

• How easy or difficult do you think it is for most Christians to believe Jesus is ready to say those things about (and to) them? Because...

• How easy or difficult is it for *you* to believe Jesus is ready to say those things about (and to) you? Why is that?

Carl Jung wrote in *Modern Man in Search of a Soul*:

> The acceptance of oneself is the essence of the whole moral problem and the epitome of a whole outlook on life. That I feed the hungry, that I forgive an insult, that I love my enemy in the name of Christ—all these are undoubtedly great virtues. What I do unto the least of my brethren, that I do unto Christ. But what if I should discover that the least amongst them all, the poorest of all the beggars, the most impudent of all the offenders, the very enemy himself—that these are within me, and that I myself stand in need of the alms of my own kindness—that I myself am the enemy who must be loved—what then? As a rule, the Christian's attitude is then reversed; there is no longer any question of love or longsuffering; we say to the brother within us "Raca," and condemn and rage against ourselves. We hide it from the world; we refuse to admit ever having met this least among the lowly in ourselves.
>
> ———————
>
> C. J. Jung, *Modern Man in Search of a Soul* (New York: Harcourt, Brace and World Harvest Books, 1933), p. 235.

Conclude by inviting your group to dive further into this subject with the *A Moveable Feast* handout or by working through **page 143** in the Student Journal.

NEW | Calling Your Bluff (20 minutes)

The Big Idea: How God uses failure to accomplish higher purposes.

Read John 4:1-30 and 39-42 with your students, then use the following questions for discussion. *(Verses 31-38 are an aside that's important, but not critical to the story we're following here.)*

You'll need—
• Bibles
• Copies of the *Calling Your Bluff* handout (on DVD) or Student Journal (**page 145**)
• Pencils

Q: Why do you suppose Jesus struck up a conversation with this woman?

• What do you think he had to gain or lose by talking with her?

• What do you think she had to gain or lose by talking with him?

FYI: When John tells us "Jews do not associate with Samaritans," he's understating the case. A Jew who used a drinking vessel that had been touched by a Samaritan was presumed to be unclean because Jews believed that the Samaritans themselves were unclean.

Q: Why do you think the insight Jesus had into this woman's life grabbed her attention so dramatically?

• Why do you think the people in town reacted so strongly to her claim that she met a man who told her everything she ever did?

Q: Have you ever seen God use this kind of messenger to reach people? If so, can you tell us the story?

Explain: **Here's what it looks like from here. It looks like forgiven people come in two flavors:**

> **1. The ones who feel so grateful to be forgiven that they stop judging other people and—like Jesus—become a friend of sinners.**

> **2. Those who seem to feel like they somehow deserve to be forgiven (some kind of exemption for special people, apparently). They become very hard to live with because they're always pointing a finger at people who do bad things or fail to do good things.**

Is it just me or does it look that way to you as well? Let's talk about that.

Q: Which of those two kinds of Christians do you prefer to hang with? Because…

• Which kind of Christian do you think is more inviting to people like the woman in John chapter 4?

Q: How do you think people become the kind of Christian you want to hang with?

• How do you think people become the other kind of Christian?

• What do you think we can do to encourage each other to become the best sort of forgiven people?

Conclude by inviting your group to dig deeper with the *Calling Your Bluff* handout or by working through **page 145** in the Student Journal.

NEW | Falling...and Bouncing Back (20 minutes)

The Big Idea: Truth, consequences, repentance, and restoration

Explain: Recap the story in 2 Samuel 11 and 12. Then ask—

I heard the story of Nathan's intervention hundreds of times before I really came to appreciate 2 Samuel 12:25. David experiences a divine do-over that comes full circle; the very man who said "you are the man" doesn't desert David. Instead, Nathan sticks around to celebrate son number two.

I love this story. It's partly why my husband and I named our son Nathan.
— KP

Q: What do you imagine David experienced, thought, and felt in the course of all that?

• While he was using his power to take Bathsheba for himself...

• When she got pregnant...

• When he arranged for the murder of her husband...

• When Nathan intervened...

• When the baby was sick...

• After the baby died...

• When Solomon was born...

Q: Have you ever seen these processes at work in someone you know? If so, and without incriminating anyone, talk about what you saw.

Explain: **I want to read two Psalms that David wrote while falling and bouncing back.**

Read Psalms 32 and 51 together.

Q: What stands out for you in these passages?

• Why do you think that strikes you?

Q: Talk about why you think David is or isn't sincere in what he wrote here.

• Have you ever felt any of the emotions he writes about here?

• If so, can you talk about that?

Q: What do these psalms reveal about what David learned from his wrongdoing and God's mercy?

• Which of these lessons is most significant to you? Because…

Conclude by recommending your students spend time privately with the *Falling… and Bouncing Back* handout or **page 146** in the Student Journal

NEW | Craving Salt (20 minutes)

The Big Idea: How to deal with a lingering taste for the old life.

Explain: **It seems like whatever happens, God helps Abraham. As the fortunes of everyone around him rise and fall, Abraham grows more prosperous. When Abraham gets in trouble (even when it's his own fault), God rescues him. It's a remarkable relationship. Abraham's nephew Lot, on the other hand, has always acted like a bum. Now—when there's about to be big trouble in Sodom and Gomorrah—God chooses to let Abraham in on it before it happens.**

Read Genesis 18:20–19:29 together, then ask—

Q: Why did God tell Abraham what he was going to do with Sodom and Gomorrah?

> You'll need—
> • Bibles
> • Paper
> • Pencils
> • Supplies for making a small, controlled fire in a metal container (play it safe and check your church or organization's policy on this)

Q: God appears to be seriously angry at Sodom and Gomorrah. What does that seem to be about?

> FYI: In an ironic twist, in Genesis 19:30-38, Lot's daughters get him drunk and sleep with him.

Explain: **Lot seems like a loser to me. I mean what kind of a guy offers his daughters to an angry mob of men so the mob can have sex with the girls? Still, God gives Lot and his family a way to escape the judgment on Sodom and Gomorrah.**

Q: Who turns out to be the biggest loser (at least in this part of the story)?

Continue: **I read this story recently about a college guy who was a believer but kept talking about his old life before he met Christ. He seemed to dwell on the past so much that his friends nicknamed him "Salty" in honor of Lot's wife. I think she was turned into a pillar of salt because her heart longed to be back in that place.**

Q: Do you sometimes feel yourself looking back at your old life and how fun it would be to be back there—or are you relieved to be out of whatever you were in?

• Maybe your old life wasn't anything you'd want to go back to. Maybe you look at the lives of some of your friends and secretly—or not so secretly—long to do the things they do. What do you think God would say about that?

Distribute paper and pencils.

Conclude by inviting everyone to make a private list of longings they'd like to surrender to God.

Collect the sheets, take them outside, and burn them in a small, controlled fire in a metal container.

As you watch the smoke of those longings rise, pray that the Spirit will enable you all to release your longings to God.

NEW | You Want Me to Marry a What? (20 minutes)

The Big Idea: How far is God willing to go to prove his love? Farther than you might think.

Explain: **The book of the prophet Hosea records a strange tale that occurred after Israel was divided into two kingdoms, Judah and Israel. You can follow along in Hosea 1–3.**

Tell the story, then ask—

Q: First, the big picture: What does God seem to be up to here?

Explain: **Priests served in the temple; prophets worked more or less in the streets. Hosea was a prophet, not a priest. Which is good, I guess, because God asked him to do things that would get a priest fired.**

> You'll need—
> • Bibles
> • Copies of the *You Want Me to Marry a What?* handout (on DVD) or Student Journal (**page 148**)
> • Pencils
> • In advance look at Hosea 1–3 and be prepared to give a brief recap of this strange tale.

Read Leviticus 21:5-15.

Q: What do you suppose the priests thought about all the goings-on in Hosea's household?

> FYI: The story of Hosea parallels that of Israel at the time of Hosea. The Israelites had been disloyal to God, worshiping Canaanite deities and thanking those gods (little "g" gods) for their blessings. And yet God still loved his people and wanted to take them back, just as Hosea took back Gomer.

• How do you imagine Hosea felt about being drawn into such weird public drama?

• How about Gomer? What do you imagine she thought and felt about all this?

Q: Suppose someone in our community said: "You're probably not going to believe this, but God told me to marry a sex worker to demonstrate how disappointed God is with his people and how much he loves them anyway." What do you think would happen around here?

Q: How do you imagine Hosea and Gomer's family story played out?

Q: What does this story suggest to you about God and do-overs?

Conclude by inviting your group to think more about this story by working through the *You Want Me to Marry a What?* handout or **page 148** in the Student Journal.

Here are some possible scenarios for what happened to Gomer and Hosea later:
• They all lived happily ever after...
• Gomer ended up going back to her old ways...
• Hosea couldn't put it behind him and spent the rest of his life punishing Gomer...
• They struggled, and their kids went a little nuts for a while, but they pulled through in the end...

HOW | Picture This (30 minutes)

The Big Idea: It may not happen quickly, but eventually there's freedom from sexual pain.

Distribute the *Picture This* handout or direct the group to **page 149** in the Student Journal.

You'll need—
- Paper
- Pencils
- Pens
- Markers
- Butcher paper on a table or posted on a wall
- Play-Doh
- Whatever else you can scrounge together that's artsy or craftsy
- Empty table for display
- Copies of the *Picture This* handout (on DVD) or Student Journal (**page 149**)

Explain: **Let's take the next five minutes to work on this privately. Then we'll talk about it a bit.**

Talk through the questions on the handout.

Explain: **We're going to take the next 15 minutes** (or whatever length of time you think is appropriate in your group) **to reflect on where we've caused or experienced sexual pain.**

Please write, draw, sculpt, tag the graffiti wall—do whatever makes sense to you as a way to express your need for do-overs because of your own sexual wrongdoing or the wrong that's been done to you.

Continue: **If you feel the need to keep that private, you're welcome to do so. There's an area for private reflection in that corner of the room.**

I'll call us back together in about 15 minutes. At that time you can display what you've created or keep it private if you need to.

When you think people are finished or when it's time to move on, give everyone a chance to look at what's been publicly displayed. (Even if there's just one thing displayed and everyone else chooses to keep their expressions private, this can still be a remarkable experience.)

Q: What was it like for you to express yourself over the last few minutes? Talk about that.

• How close did you get to the reality of what's been done to harm you or what you've done to harm someone else?

Q: Do you think you have any unfinished business? Can you talk about that?

• What do you think you need to do next?

Q: How do you hope God will be involved in this process?

• What other help do you think you could use?

• What do you think you may have to gain or lose by getting help?

Conclude by asking, **What would you like us to pray for you?**

Then take a few minutes to pray together—asking for God's helping and giving thanks for what God has already done.

THE STUFF AT THE BACK OF THE BOOK

Plumbing + Wiring FAQs

Don't hate us. We didn't ask the questions; we're just trying to respond honestly. So skip the ones you think are obvious and be glad there's somebody out there who knows less than you. At the end of every answer, feel free to circle whether you knew it or didn't know it.

Q: Is there a right way to kiss?

Uh, lip-to-lip works pretty well. The truth is that kissing comes pretty naturally for most people, and the rest catch on with a little practice. We found the back of the hand, pressing the thumb against the first finger, is a reasonably good place to work on technique…just kidding…okay we really did that, but only a couple of times, and never in front of a mirror. Sometimes noses get bumped and braces get locked up, but those mishaps are rare. ***Knew it/Didn't know it***

Q: How do people breathe when they kiss?

Although the mouth is pretty preoccupied during kissing, the nose usually isn't—nor should it be—making kissing more difficult, but not impossible, during the cold and flu season. ***Knew it/Didn't know it***

Q: What exactly happens during sex?

Technically, the sexual act proceeds through several phases. The first is an excitement phase, marked by an increase in pulse and blood pressure as blood rushes to the surface of the body. Genital fluids are also secreted during the excitement phase (for both the guy and girl), and the vagina expands (that would be the girl only—just to clarify). The next phase is the plateau phase, which is pretty brief and may conclude with an orgasm. The third phase is the resolution phase, during which the girl's and the guy's bodies return to normal. **Knew it/Didn't know it**

Q: What's an orgasm?

An orgasm, also called a *climax*, is the peak of physical sexual excitement and gratification. Physically, it's marked by a faster pulse, higher blood pressure, intensely pleasurable sensations in the genitalia, and spasms of the pelvic muscles that cause contractions in the girl's vagina and sperm ejaculation from the guy's penis. Emotionally, it is marked by an overwhelming feeling of pleasure and release. Depending on who you're having sex with, it might also be a guilty pleasure—a mix of "I can't believe how good that felt" and "I can't believe how bad I feel about how good that felt." **Knew it/Didn't know it**

> I used to think I'd just want to have sex 24 hours a day. I didn't know that the body parts just get tired and sore after a while. I didn't know that sometimes I'd just be too tired to care about it and just want to go to sleep.
> —Hanna, on the information she got about sex

Q: Does an orgasm always happen during intercourse?

Not always. Sometimes the guy and girl feel fairly aroused and have a grand ole time together, but neither (or only one) will actually have an orgasm. It's also possible to have an orgasm before or after sexual intercourse. **Knew it/Didn't know it**

Q: Is an orgasm different for a guy than for a girl?

Well, yes, because they have different body parts. Both experience quick, rapid muscular contractions, but the girl's usually last longer. The girl can often have several orgasms, one right after another, while the guy usually has to wait a while (like several hours). However, since the guy usually becomes aroused more quickly, he has orgasms more consistently during sexual intercourse. **Knew it/Didn't know it**

Q: Do orgasms always feel the same?

No. They're almost always good, but sometimes they're really great. Often how great it is relates to how connected you're feeling to your partner, how physically fresh and aroused you are, how mentally focused or distracted you are, and how emotionally free you feel to enjoy what's going on. **Knew it/Didn't know it**

Q: How long does an orgasm take?

Although the orgasm is the most talked about phase in sexual intercourse, it's actually pretty short, ranging from five to 30 seconds. **Knew it/Didn't know it**

Q: What's an erection?

When a guy becomes sexually aroused by physical or psychological stimulation, the blood flowing into his penis is increased and the blood flowing out of his penis is temporarily reduced. As a result, the tissue swells and the penis is enlarged, hardened, and elevated. **Knew it/Didn't know it**

Q: I've heard that alcohol will help your sex drive, but I've also heard it will hurt it. What's the deal?

Alcohol is a depressant, so it tends to reduce inhibitions and dull decision-making skills. So people who've had something to drink may be more flirtatious or willing to try things they wouldn't even consider when they were sober. Because of this, some people jump to the conclusion that alcohol increases sex drive. But actually, alcohol depresses the nervous system and diminishes muscular coordination and nerve sensation. Sober sex is generally more pleasurable than sex under the influence. Perhaps the biggest gotcha is that the risk of pregnancy and sexually transmitted infections is increased by carelessness, so re-read the first sentence and do the math. **Knew it/Didn't know it**

Q: Does sex hurt?

Vaginal sex can be painful—especially the first few times, and especially for women. Imagine going dancing for the first time. Since you don't know what you're doing and you haven't practiced, you might hurt yourself or your partner. The same is true for sex when you're new at it. This is one reason why "wham, bam, thank you ma'am" encounters are generally disappointing for women, while the patient, caring, unhurried touch of someone who's not in a rush because you're married for life can make the experience go more smoothly right from the start. ***Knew it/Didn't know it***

Anal penetration is another thing altogether, and it can be quite painful. Unlike the vagina, the anus isn't very elastic, doesn't secret sexual fluids to lubricate the opening, and is more subject to abrasions and tearing (not weeping; small rips in the tissue). Abrasions and tears make anal penetration far more risky than vaginal sex for the transmission of bacterial and viral diseases. ***Knew it/Didn't know it***

Q: Does the size of a penis matter?

Most guys assume the average size of an erect penis is six inches, and then they get worried because theirs is smaller than that. However, the reality is that an erect penis is usually around 5.1 or 5.2 inches, and a non-erect (or flaccid) penis is 3.5 inches. Regardless of penis size, a guy really doesn't need to worry about it. In a miracle of creative design, the girl's body adjusts to fit whatever size he is. ***Knew it/Didn't know it***

Q: Is masturbation wrong?

Ah, that's a biggie. Masturbation, or stimulating your own genitals for pleasure, has both fans and critics. Some people believe it's wrong all the time, others believe it's right almost all of the time, and still others fall somewhere in the middle, arguing that occasional masturbation is okay, as long as it isn't fueled by lustful fantasies and doesn't become a disruptive, self-absorbed preoccupation (which happens to more people than you might think—or maybe it happens to fewer people than you might think—depending on what you might think). We fall somewhere in the middle. For more about masturbation, see Session 4, "Desire." ***Knew it/Didn't know it***

Q: What is oral sex?

Contrary to early reports, oral sex is not talking about sex. Who knew? Instead, it means using the mouth to stimulate another person's genital organs. Also contrary to early reports, sexual infections are transmitted fairly easily through cuts, abrasions, tears, and sores in and around the mouth. ***Knew it/Didn't know it***

Q: Is oral sex the same as sex?

Well, babies can't be conceived during oral sex, if that's what you're asking. But we're inclined to say that anything that includes the word *sex*—vaginal sex, anal sex, oral sex—is sex. And don't think that dropping the word *sex*—"Oh we only do oral," or "I only do anal"—changes the substance of the behavior. The exchange of body fluids is a pretty reliable clue. Sexual gratification is another clue. As one of our friends admitted after breaking off a relationship with a married person who kept offering assurances that they weren't really having sex: "No, we didn't have intercourse...but an orgasm is an orgasm, so..." We didn't know about the affair until it was over and our friend was trying to make amends—hoping for do-overs from an emotionally damaging mistake. ***Knew it/Didn't know it***

Q: What if my breasts are different sizes?

That's just how some girls are. There's nothing wrong with it, especially when your breasts are still developing; however, if you notice any lumps in them, you should have a medical doctor look at them just to make sure it's not a tumor or a cyst. ***Knew it/Didn't know it***

Q: What if my testicles are different sizes?

That's just how some guys are. If the larger testicle is hard, a guy should have it checked out by a medical doctor to make sure it's not a cyst, tumor, or hernia. ***Knew it/Didn't know it***

Q: What are wet dreams, and why do they happen?

Wet dreams are also known as *nocturnal emissions*. Starting at puberty, as a guy's body begins to mature, he's likely to have involuntary emissions of semen from his penis during sleep. Nocturnal emissions sometimes accompany sexually stimulating dreams—hence the term *wet dream*. ***Knew it/Didn't know it***

Q: Have I done something wrong if I have a wet dream?

Some guys feel guilty about wet dreams—maybe because they remind them of when they used to wet the bed or maybe because they're dreaming about specific girls or women when the emission occurs. However, it's just a natural, subconscious event that doesn't necessarily mean anything. ***Knew it/Didn't know it***

Q: If the guy withdraws before he ejaculates, can the girl still get pregnant?

During extended foreplay, a small amount of pre-ejaculatory fluid seeps from a guy's penis. This fluid contains real, live, and active sperm that can get the girl pregnant. Because of this, withdrawing the penis from the vagina before ejaculation is not generally considered reliable birth control. **Knew it/Didn't know it**

Q: And what exactly is *foreplay*?

Foreplay is the early stage of sex that gets people ready for the main event. In other words, making out is foreplay. This explains why people get all worked up and frustrated when they make out—and why they're tempted to move on to the main event prematurely. **Knew it/Didn't know it**

Q: I've heard that a girl won't get pregnant if she has sex standing up or if she has sex in a hot tub. Is that true?

The girl can be jumping up and down, doing handstands, cartwheels, or backflips. If the guy introduces sperm into her vagina, she could get pregnant. The position doesn't matter and neither does her environment. She can be in a hot tub, sauna, submarine, or spacecraft—if she's having vaginal sex, she could get pregnant at any time. **Knew it/Didn't know it**

Q: Does having sex change you physically?

The biggest change is that if you're a girl, you could get pregnant. Also for girls, a physical membrane called the *hymen* (a sheet-like lining just inside the vagina) can break, which might hurt and cause some bleeding. For guys nothing really changes physically. Either gender can pick up or pass along a sexually transmitted disease at any time (including the first time). Oh yeah, and did we mention that if you're a girl, you could get pregnant? We don't mean to harp, but that's a pretty huge change. **Knew it/Didn't know it**

Q: Why am I hearing so much now about the HPV vaccine? What is it? Should I get it?

Coming up with an answer to the first question isn't all that hard, although the answer varies by gender. In 2007, the U.S. Food and Drug Administration released a vaccine developed to prevent cervical cancer and other diseases in females caused by certain types of human papilloma virus (HPV) transmitted by genital, anal, or oral contact. This vaccine (called Gardasil) protects against four types of HPV, which together create 70% of cervical cancers and 90% of genital warts in females.

At the time of the writing of this curriculum, there is no HPV vaccine for males. Yet given that HPV's effects on guys can include genital warts, as well as penile, anal, and throat cancer, there is more conversation about someday (maybe not even all that far away) offering a corresponding vaccine for guys.

So if you're a female, should you get the vaccine that's available to you? That question is trickier. The FDA licensed this vaccine for girls and women ages 9 to 26, and it's more effective before women become sexually active. Some folks believe that getting the vaccine might encourage girls (and guys, for that matter) to engage in premature sexual activity. Others believe it's important to get the vaccine even if you plan to remain abstinent because you might not live up to your plan, or there might be circumstances beyond your control—meaning sexual assault. Whether or not you get the vaccine is something you should talk over with your parents and other wise adults who know you well. **Knew it/Didn't know it**

Q: Will I get AIDS if I'm around someone who has it?

According to the U.S. Centers for Disease Control and Prevention, HIV (Human Immunodeficiency Virus, the virus that causes AIDS, or Acquired Immunodeficiency Syndrome) isn't transmitted through day-to-day activities such as shaking hands, hugging, or a casual kiss. Nor can you become infected from a toilet seat, drinking fountain, doorknob, dishes, food, or pets. HIV is primarily found in the blood, semen, or vaginal fluid of an infected person and can be transmitted by having sex (anal, vaginal, or oral), sharing contaminated needles, during pregnancy, or through breast-feeding. **Knew it/Didn't know it**

Q: Sex is always neat and clean in the movies—is that right?

Sex is messy—not gross, necessarily, but messy. When the guy ejaculates, the two to six milliliters of semen containing about 300,000,000 sperm has to go somewhere. Plus the girl's vagina builds up additional lubrication. You figure it out.
Knew it/Didn't know it

Q: Christians are so prudish. They must have lousy sex, right?

Actually, quite the opposite, if a national survey of 3,500 Americans ages 18 to 59 is to be believed. According to this 1994 survey, Protestant Christian women are most likely to achieve orgasm each and every time they have vaginal intercourse.[36] Could this be a fringe benefit of following Christ? **Knew it/Didn't know it**

36. Philip Elmer-Dewitt, "Now for the Truth About Americans and Sex," *Time*. (October 17, 1994), http://www.time.com/time/magazine/article/0,9171,981624,00.html (accessed July 31, 2008).

Back-to-Basics Biology

This is a cheat sheet on basic sexual biology. Use it to refresh your memory from health class. (This won't be on the test.) Feel free to circle whether you knew it or didn't know it.

Clitoris—Apparently the only organ in the human anatomy designed solely for experiencing sexual stimuli, the clitoris of a female is a two- to three-centimeter long funnel loaded with nerve endings. It's very sensitive to both pleasure and pain. *Knew it/Didn't know it*

Coronal ridge—The bulge near the end of the penis. *Knew it/Didn't know it*

Glans (or head)—If a male has been circumcised, the glans is located at the end of the penis. If a male hasn't been circumcised, the glans is covered with a loose skin called the foreskin. *Knew it/Didn't know it*

Labia majora—A part of the vulva that protects the rest of the vagina. If a female hasn't given birth, then the outer lips of the labia majora probably meet at the center of her genitals. *Knew it/Didn't know it*

Ovaries—The ovaries are female internal organs shaped like large almonds. They're located on either side of the uterus and produce some of the sex hormones that affect the menstrual cycle. Their primary function, however, is to release one of about 400,000 eggs for reproduction 14 days before a girl's period begins. The egg is either fertilized by a guy's sperm and becomes implanted in the uterus, or it's discharged from the body with the menstrual blood flow. This process begins in puberty and continues until menopause. *Knew it/Didn't know it*

Penis—The penis is the external male organ for sexual intercourse and the method by which sperm is introduced into a female's vagina. During sexual excitement, blood is temporarily trapped in the chambers of the erectile tissue in the penis, causing the penis to become enlarged, firm, and erect. *Knew it/Didn't know it*

Scrotum—A pouch in the male anatomy that holds two glands called the testes. *Knew it/Didn't know it*

Seminal vesicles—glands that secrete many of the components of semen into the vas deferens (keep reading to find out what a vas deferens is). *Knew it/Didn't know it*

Shaft—The cylindrical structure of the penis. ***Knew it/Didn't know it***

Sperm—Cells from a male that are capable of fertilizing a mature egg in a female reproductive system. The process of sexual arousal and ejaculation activates the otherwise immobile cells so they become self-propelled in the seminal fluid by means of a tiny tail that whips from side to side. Sperm are available more or less on demand in quantities of around 300,000,000 cells per ejaculation. Under favorable conditions sperm live about three days after ejaculation. ***Knew it/Didn't know it***

Testes—The testes (the primary male reproductive organ) are two small balls that move around in the scrotum and generate sperm. ***Knew it/Didn't know it***

Urethra—The thin tube that carries urine from the male bladder—or sperm from the seminal vesicles—through the penis. ***Knew it/Didn't know it***

Uterus (also called the womb)—A pear-shaped muscular organ in the female reproductive system, located between the urinary bladder and rectum, that connects through the cervix to the vagina. The lining of the uterus—the endometrium—secretes fluids that keep eggs and sperm alive and nourishes fertilized eggs. If a mature egg isn't fertilized, then it's flushed out with the endometrium through the vagina during monthly menstruation. ***Knew it/Didn't know it***

Vagina—The vagina (the muscular canal leading from the vulva to the uterus) changes in size to receive any size penis during intercourse and expands to accommodate a baby during delivery. ***Knew it/Didn't know it***

Vas deferens—The duct through which sperm moves from the testicle to the urethra. ***Knew it/Didn't know it***

Vulva—The external female genitalia that surround the opening to the vagina. ***Knew it/Didn't know it***

How to Help Victims of Sexual Abuse and Other Tough Stuff

If you make your room the least bit safe, there's a better than fair chance some kid will come out with something shocking. If that happens, you'll have to decide in real time the degree to which you'll deal with whatever he said right then and there and what you think should be reserved for a private conversation after the meeting.

If a kid reveals things about her sexual experience that are troubling, frightening, or even dangerous, don't panic. Chances are if someone chooses to trust you with a difficult story about sexual abuse, then she won't be going off the deep end any time soon. In fact, she may be telling you to *keep* from going off the deep end. She's probably silently carried the story for a while already, and you've given her the impression you can help.

You can. You can't *solve* anything, but you can help her get the help she needs. So, don't freak out. Take a deep breath, express your sympathy, and listen like crazy.

If, after you hear a student's story, you believe that a reasonable person would call it sexual abuse, chances are—and that's about 99 chances out of a hundred, so you should assume this applies to you—you are what most states call a "Mandated Reporter." That means that if you have convincing evidence of sexual abuse, the law requires you to report it. (No kidding; this is not a suggestion or a guideline—it's a *mandate* to report a crime.)

If you're not sure how to do that, here's a path:

I don't know whether I heard this somewhere or just recognized the pattern; I only know there was a shift in the depth and breadth of my work with adolescents when I figured out that almost any significant adolescent issue I mentioned in a serious manner was followed—usually pretty quickly—by a student who wanted to talk with me about that. I never knew a kid struggling with an eating disorder until I mentioned in a youth group talk that a lot of people struggle with eating disorders. After that I never ran out of people who wanted help with an eating disorder. The same is true of sexual abuse in all its forms, sexual identity issues, violence, substance addictions and sexual compulsions. Adolescents (and their siblings and parents, for that matter) are looking for open doors. I would rather they walk through our doors than some others I can think of.
— Jim Hancock, *The Youth Worker's Guide to Helping Teenagers in Crisis*

Rich Van Pelt and Jim Hancock, *The Youth Worker's Guide to Helping Teenagers in Crisis* (Grand Rapids, Mich.: Youth Specialties/Zondervan, 2005), p. 187.

• Begin with the senior staff member in your church or organization. That person will probably know how to proceed. If you're convinced the situation is real but your staff leader seems confused or you fear he'll sweep it under the rug, be sure you take the next steps.

• Call the head counselor or vice principal at your local school. Explain the situation to the best of your understanding and ask for help to understand your legal responsibilities. There's a pretty good chance that person will either take it from there (she's a Mandated Reporter, too, and she's almost certainly been down this road before) or offer to help you make the report. In the (highly) unlikely event the kid is lying, the school official will be a good backup.

• Call or visit the sheriff, police, or Child Protective Services (whatever that may be called where you live). Law enforcement jurisdictions can be confusing, and it's easy to get lost in the system. It's a safe bet that school personnel have already been through this—they'll walk you through it if you ask humbly.

• Get in touch with a trustworthy counselor or therapist and ask her to be a resource to you.

• If you go through all of these channels and you believe nothing is happening, start again at the top, humbly express your frustration, and ask for help. Be the widow in Luke 18 who keeps coming to the judge for justice until he pays attention. You're a poor youth worker looking for justice in a system where you probably don't feel at home. That's okay. Keep after it. They'll listen to you eventually—if you don't give up. But don't showboat. Don't parade around city hall or call press conferences to put people on the spot. You're most likely to get through the system by building relationships, not tearing them down.

Then:

• Stay close to the victimized adolescent. Revealing the sordid details of an abusive relationship is a gruesome ordeal for almost anyone. In many cases these days, multidisciplinary intervention teams from Child Protective Services (CPS) are responsible for reducing the trauma kids suffer as a result of a crime against them. The CPS team is trained for the legal, psychological, and familial aspects of a thorough investigation. The result is that kids are spared the agony of having to tell their horror story over and over again to a host of different people. But don't depend on that. Do what it takes to remain close for the duration.

• Be alert for signs of self-injurious behavior. Once they've told someone about abuse, it's not unusual for young people to enter a period of high risk for suicide, drug abuse, and other self-destructive behaviors. Families don't always respond the way we hope. Instead of surrounding the victim with loving concern, families sometimes respond in disbelief, anger, shock, or paralysis, leaving the child unsupported. Step into the gap; "come alongside" with God's love, comfort, and assurance.

Finally:

• Prepare for next time by picking up a copy of *The Youth Worker's Guide to Helping Teenagers in Crisis* (Rich Van Pelt and Jim Hancock, Youth Specialties/Zondervan, 2005). Pay special attention to the sections on Pregnancy, Incest, Sexual Abuse, Rape, Sexual Identity Issues, Cutting and Self-Injurious Behavior, Eating Disorders, Sexual Abuse, and Referral.

• Teach your students to send or bring their friends to you for help. Help them identify the staff member at school who's most likely to pitch in if they need help fast.

• In case you're not available and it's a weekend and they need advice RIGHT NOW, give them **800-4-A-CHILD** (800.422.4453), the number for **Childhelp USA®**. These folks specialize in sexual abuse assistance.

• And give them the **Girls and Boys Town Hotline** number (**800.448.3000**) as well. It's a good go-to resource in a pinch. They're not just knowledgeable about defusing emotional time bombs; they also have a terrific database of helping resources in every area code.

All the Sex in the Bible

By Bible Passage

Genesis 1:28   reproduction
Genesis 2:24   one flesh
Genesis 4:1   Adam and Eve
Genesis 4:17   Cain and his wife
Genesis 16:1-16   Abraham, Sarah, and Hagar
Genesis 19:1-29   Sodom and Gomorrah
Genesis 19:30-35   Lot and his daughters
Genesis 29:21-30   Jacob, Leah, and Rachel
Genesis 34:1-31   Dinah's rape and rescue
Genesis 30:1-24   Leah and Rachel's maidservants and Jacob
Genesis 35:22   Reuben and his father's concubine
Genesis 38:1-30   Tamar and her in-laws
Genesis 39:1-21   Joseph and Potiphar's wife

Exodus 19:15   abstinence
Exodus 22:16   sleeping around
Exodus 22:19   sex with animals

Leviticus 15:16-17   wet dreams
Leviticus 15:18   sexual hygiene
Leviticus 15:19-28   sexual hygiene for females
Leviticus 18:6-13   incest
Leviticus 18:14-18   sleeping around
Leviticus 18:19   abstinence during a woman's period
Leviticus 18:20-21   sleeping around
Leviticus 18:22   homosexuality
Leviticus 18:23   sex with animals
Leviticus 18:24-30   consequences of sex acts listed in verses 6-23
Leviticus 19:20   sleeping around
Leviticus 19:29   prostitution in the family
Leviticus 20:10-12   consequences of sleeping around
Leviticus 20:13   consequences of homosexuality
Leviticus 20:15-16   consequences of sex with animals

Leviticus 20:17, 19-20	consequences of incest
Leviticus 20:18	abstinence during a woman's period
Leviticus 20:21	sex with in-laws
Leviticus 22:4	sexual hygiene for males
Numbers 5:11-31	handling suspicions about spouse's adultery
Numbers 25:1-3	spiritual side effect of sleeping around
Deuteronomy 22:13-21	divorce after consummation
Deuteronomy 22:22-24	consequences of sleeping around
Deuteronomy 22:25-29	consequences of rape
Deuteronomy 23:10-11	wet dreams
Deuteronomy 24:5	marital sex the first year
Deuteronomy 25:5-10	sex to carry on the family name
Deuteronomy 27:20	consequences of sleeping with a stepmother
Deuteronomy 27:21	consequences of bestiality
Deuteronomy 27:22	consequences of incest
Deuteronomy 27:23	consequences of sleeping with an in-law
Judges 16:1	Samson and a prostitute
Judges 16:4-20	Samson and Delilah
Judges 19:16-30	rape of a concubine
Ruth 4:13	Boaz and Ruth
1 Samuel 1:19-20	Elkanah and Hannah
1 Samuel 2:22	Eli's sons and the church women
2 Samuel 11:2-5	David and Bathsheba (first sexual encounter)
2 Samuel 11:11	Uriah and abstinence from marital sex
2 Samuel 12:11	Nathan's prophecy about David's concubines
2 Samuel 12:24	David and Bathsheba (marital sex)
2 Samuel 13:1-22	rape of Tamar
2 Samuel 16:20-22	Absalom and David's concubines
1 Chronicles 2:21	Hezron and the daughter of Makir
1 Chronicles 7:23	Ephraim and his wife

Proverbs 2:11-19	wisdom as a safeguard against seduction
Proverbs 5:1-20	dangers of sleeping around versus pleasures of married sex
Proverbs 6:20-35	wisdom as a safeguard against seduction
Proverbs 7:1-27	wisdom as a safeguard against seduction
Proverbs 23:26-28	warning about prostitutes
Song of Songs	romantic poetry of marital sex
Isaiah 8:3	Isaiah and his wife
Isaiah 57:5	lusting
Jeremiah 2:20	Israel compared to a prostitute
Jeremiah 3:1-20	allegorical sex escapades of Israel and Judah
Ezekiel 16:1-42	allegory of wife becoming prostitute
Ezekiel 23:1-49	allegory of two promiscuous sisters
Hosea 1:2	Hosea and adulterous wife
Hosea 2:2-15	allegorical lust and sleeping around
Hosea 3:1-3	Hosea buys back his wife after prostitution
Hosea 4:10-19	consequences of physical and spiritual prostitution
Hosea 8:9	metaphor of Israel as a prostitute
Hosea 9:1	metaphor of Israel as a prostitute
Nahum 3:4	metaphor of Assyria as a prostitute
Matthew 5:27-30	lust and adultery
Matthew 15:19	source of sexual sin
Matthew 19:5	becoming one flesh
Matthew 19:9	divorce and sleeping around
Mark 7:21	source of sexual sin
John 4:16	woman at the well
John 8:3-11	Jesus and the adulterous woman
Acts 15:20, 29	sexual sin
Acts 21:25	sexual sin

Romans 1:24-27	lust and homosexuality
Romans 13:13-14	safeguard against orgies and sexual sin
1 Corinthians 5:1-2	Paul's reaction to sexual sin
1 Corinthians 6:9-10	consequences of sleeping around, prostitution, and homosexuality
1 Corinthians 6:12-20	fleeing sexual sin and prostitutes
1 Corinthians 7:2-5	sexual gratification and abstinence in marriage
1 Corinthians 7:9	lust and staying single
1 Corinthians 10:8	consequences of sleeping around
2 Corinthians 12:21	Paul's reaction to sexual sin
Galatians 5:19-21	source and consequences of sexual sin
Ephesians 5:3	warning against sleeping around
Ephesians 5:31	husband and wife as one flesh
Colossians 3:5	warning against lust and sleeping around
1 Thessalonians 4:3-5	God's view of lust and sexual sin
James 1:13-15	metaphor of sin as seduction
Jude 1:7	example of Sodom and Gomorrah
Revelation 2:14	Balaam, Balak, and sexual sin
Revelation 2:20-22	allegorical sleeping around (for the church of Thyatira)
Revelation 9:21	sexual sin
Revelation 17:1-2	allegorical "great prostitute"
Revelation 18:2-3, 9	allegory of Babylon, the great prostitute
Revelation 19:1-2	allegory of Babylon, the great prostitute
Revelation 21:8	sexual sin and the lake of fire
Revelation 22:15	sexual sin and Christ's return

By Topic

abstinence

Exodus 19:15
1 Corinthians 7:2-5

allegorical sex

Jeremiah 2:20
Jeremiah 3:1-20
Ezekiel 16:1-42
Ezekiel 23:1-49
Hosea 2:2-15
Hosea 8:9
Hosea 9:1
Nahum 3:4
Ephesians 5:31
James 1:13-15
Revelation 2:20-22
Revelation 17:1-2
Revelation 18:2-3, 9
Revelation 19:1-2

ancient Hebrew sexual hygiene

Leviticus 15:16-28
Leviticus 18:19
Leviticus 20:18
Leviticus 22:4
Deuteronomy 23:10-11

consequences of sexual sin

Genesis 19:1-29
Exodus 22:16
Exodus 22:19
Leviticus 18:6-30
Leviticus 19:29
Leviticus 20:12-13, 15-22
Numbers 5:11-31
Numbers 25:1-3
Deuteronomy 22:13-29
Deuteronomy 27:20-23
Judges 16:4-20
Proverbs 2:11-19
Proverbs 5:1-14
Proverbs 6:20-35
Proverbs 7:1-27
Proverbs 23:26-28
Jeremiah 3:1-20
Ezekiel 16:1-42
Ezekiel 23:1-49
Hosea 2:2-15
Hosea 4:10-19
Matthew 5:27-30
Matthew 19:9
John 8:3-11
Romans 1:24-27
1 Corinthians 6:9-10
1 Corinthians 6:12-20
1 Corinthians 10:8
Galatians 5:19-21
Ephesians 5:3
Colossians 3:5
Jude 1:7
Revelation 21:8
Revelation 22:15

divorce

Deuteronomy 22:13-21
Matthew 19:9

having children

Genesis 1:28
Genesis 4:1
Genesis 4:17
Genesis 16:1-16
Genesis 19:30-35
Genesis 30:1-24
Genesis 38:1-30
Deuteronomy 25:5-10
Ruth 4:13
1 Samuel 1:19-20
2 Samuel 11:2-5
2 Samuel 12:24
1 Chronicles 2:21
1 Chronicles 7:23
Isaiah 8:3

homosexuality

Leviticus 18:22
Leviticus 20:13
Romans 1:24-27
1 Corinthians 6:9-10

incest

Genesis 19:30-35
Leviticus 18:6-13
Deuteronomy 27:22
2 Samuel 13:1-22

lust

Genesis 19:1-29
Genesis 39:1-21
Judges 16:4-20
2 Samuel 11:2-5
Proverbs 6:20-35

Proverbs 7:1-27
Proverbs 23:26-28
Isaiah 57:5
Jeremiah 3:1-20
Ezekiel 23:1-49
Hosea 2:2-15
Nahum 3:4
Matthew 5:27-30
Romans 1:24-27
1 Corinthians 7:9
Ephesians 5:3
Colossians 3:5
1 Thessalonians 4:3-5
James 1:13-15

marital sex

Genesis 2:24
Genesis 4:1
Genesis 4:17
Genesis 29:21-30
Deuteronomy 22:13-21
Deuteronomy 24:5
Ruth 4:13
1 Samuel 1:19-20
2 Samuel 11:11
2 Samuel 12:24
1 Chronicles 2:21
1 Chronicles 7:23
Proverbs 5:15-20
Song of Songs (all)
Isaiah 8:3
Matthew 19:5
1 Corinthians 7:2-5

messy multi-marital sexual arrangements
Genesis 16:1-16
Genesis 29:21-30
Genesis 30:1-24
Genesis 38:1-30
2 Samuel 12:11

prostitution
Genesis 38:1-30
Leviticus 19:29
Judges 16:1
Proverbs 2:11-19
Proverbs 5:1-14
Proverbs 6:20-35
Proverbs 7:1-27
Proverbs 23:26-28
Jeremiah 3:1-20
Ezekiel 16:1-42
Ezekiel 23:1-49
Hosea 3:1-3
Hosea 4:10-19
Hosea 8:9
Hosea 9:1
Nahum 3:4
1 Corinthians 6:9-10
1 Corinthians 6:12-20

rape
Deuteronomy 22:25-29
Judges 19:16-30
2 Samuel 13:1-22

seduction
Genesis 19:30-35
Genesis 38:1-30
Genesis 39:1-21
Exodus 22:16
2 Samuel 11:2-5
Proverbs 2:11-19
Proverbs 5:1-20
Proverbs 6:20-35
Proverbs 7:1-27
Proverbs 23:26-28
Jeremiah 3:1-20
Ezekiel 16:1-42
Ezekiel 23:1-49
Nahum 3:4
James 1:13-15

sex with animals
Exodus 22:19
Leviticus 18:23
Leviticus 20:15-16

sleeping around
Genesis 35:22
Exodus 22:16
Leviticus 18:6-18, 20-22
Leviticus 19:20
Leviticus 20:10-13, 19-20
Numbers 5:11-31
Numbers 25:1-3
Deuteronomy 22:22-24
Deuteronomy 27:20, 23
1 Samuel 2:22
2 Samuel 11:2-5
2 Samuel 12:11
2 Samuel 16:20-22
Proverbs 5:1-20
Proverbs 6:20-35
Proverbs 7:1-27

Proverbs 23:26-28
Jeremiah 3:1-20
Ezekiel 16:1-42
Ezekiel 23:1-49
Hosea 1:2
Hosea 2:2-15
Matthew 15:19
Matthew 19:9
Mark 7:21
John 4:16
John 8:3-11
Acts 15:20, 29
Acts 21:25
Romans 1:24-27
Romans 13:13-14
1 Corinthians 5:1-2
1 Corinthians 6:9-10
1 Corinthians 6:12-20
1 Corinthians 10:8
2 Corinthians 12:21
Galatians 5:19-21
Ephesians 5:3
Colossians 3:5
1 Thessalonians 4:3-5
Jude 1:7
Revelation 2:14
Revelation 9:21
Revelation 21:8
Revelation 22:15

wet dreams
Leviticus 15:16-17
Leviticus 22:4
Deuteronomy 23:10-11

In this six-week study, you can help students deal with the thoughts and feelings they're experiencing in the midst of or after a divorce—whether it happened recently or when they were younger. With engaging stories and thought-provoking questions, students will explore issues of anger, guilt, forgiveness, family, and more through a biblical lens, offering them hope and healing.

Dealing with Divorce Leader's Guide
Finding Direction When Your Parents Split Up
Elizabeth Oates
RETAIL $14.99
ISBN 978-0-310-27887-0

Dealing with Divorce Participant's Guide
Finding Direction When Your Parents Split Up
Elizabeth Oates
RETAIL $9.99
ISBN 978-0-310-27886-3

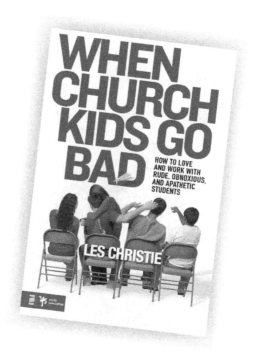

You may have an amazing program and be well connected to your students, but that doesn't always guarantee a problem-free ministry. Discipline problems and apathetic students can drive you out of youth ministry (or out of your mind!). But you don't have to let that happen. Learn how to take a positive approach to discipline in this practical book from a youth ministry veteran, and keep the chaos to a minimum.

Whether it's dodgeball in the church gym or a rock climbing trip on a summer retreat, you have precious cargo in your care, and it's your responsibility to bring them home safely and in one piece. Make sure your ministry is safe and that you're protected so you never have to be the one saying, "I never took safety seriously until…"

Better Safe Than Sued
Keeping Your Students and Ministry Alive
Jack Crabtree
RETAIL $16.99
ISBN 978-0-310-28261-7

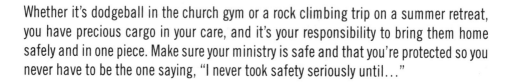

CPSIA information can be obtained
at www.ICGtesting.com
Printed in the USA
LVHW050636180223
739446LV00001B/2